Psychology and Economic Injustice

Psychology of Women
Book Series

Psychology and Economic Injustice

PERSONAL, PROFESSIONAL,
AND POLITICAL INTERSECTIONS

Bernice Lott and Heather E. Bullock

AMERICAN PSYCHOLOGICAL ASSOCIATION
WASHINGTON, DC

Published by
American Psychological Association
750 First Street, NE
Washington, DC 20002
www.apa.org

To order
APA Order Department
P.O. Box 92984
Washington, DC 20090-2984
Tel: (800) 374-2721
Direct: (202) 336-5510
Fax: (202) 336-5502
TDD/TTY: (202) 336-6123
Online: www.apa.org/books/
E-mail: order@apa.org

In the U.K., Europe, Africa, and the Middle East, copies may be ordered from
American Psychological Association
3 Henrietta Street
Covent Garden, London
WC2E 8LU England

Typeset in Minion by World Composition Services, Inc., Sterling, VA

Printer: Maple-Vail Book Manufacturing Group, Binghamton, NY
Cover Designer: Berg Design, Albany, NY
Technical/Production Editor: Harriet Kaplan

The opinions and statements published are the responsibility of the authors, and such opinions and statements do not necessarily represent the policies of the American Psychological Association.

Library of Congress Cataloging-in-Publication Data

Lott, Bernice E.
    Psychology and economic injustice : personal, professional, and political intersections / by Bernice Lott and Heather E. Bullock.
        p. cm.— (Psychology of women book series)
    Includes bibliographical references and index.
    ISBN-13: 978-1-59147-429-6
    ISBN-10: 1-59147-429-9
    1. Social classes—United States—Psychological aspects. 2. Feminist psychology—United States. 3. Poor women—United States—Psychology.
    4. Discrimination—United States. I. Bullock, Heather E. II. Title. III. Series.

HT609.L67 2006
305.5019—dc22   2006005203

British Library Cataloguing-in-Publication Data
A CIP record is available from the British Library.

Printed in the United States of America
First Edition

We dedicate this book to our parents,
Annie and Samuel, and Marilyn and Forman.

Contents

Series Foreword

Contemporary society is marked by a great number of critical challenges: The number of children and families living in poverty is rising. High school dropouts from our nation's schools are increasing, and high stakes testing is changing the way our students are being educated. We are living with the effects of welfare reform and need to look critically at how these reforms have affected children, youth, and families. Head Start programs, long celebrated for being scientifically based educational interventions, are at risk for losing funding.

Since September 11, 2001, we have lived with new restrictions on our freedoms, new costs for wars launched in the Middle East, and constant fear. How is this new anxiety affecting women who have long been the transmitters of culture and community? Mental health problems in this age of anxiety are enormous even as managed care and federal policies reduce support for mental health services. How can prevention programs be developed in an age of drastic budget cuts and removal of basic social and health services? New neurological research and the genome project are revealing individual differences that require careful thought regarding the implications for education, socialization, and remediation. While our country is becoming more diverse, tolerance and celebration of diversity is decreasing and reproductive choices are becoming more restricted. How are individual rights preserved while we balance human rights and the welfare of others?

Feminist psychologists have claimed they have a moral imperative to improve society. This book, and others to follow in the series of monographs in the Society for the Psychology of Women Series (Division 35) of the American Psychological Association, draw on the expertise of psychologists who have been working on social issues using the lens of feminist consciousness. Forthcoming books in the series will present invited monographs that address critical issues facing our society. These volumes will be based on current scholarship but will be written in a way that is accessible to lay persons who are not knowledgeable in a given field. Longer than a journal article but shorter than a full text, these invited monographs in the series will not just tell the readers *what we know* on a topic, but also what we as a society (as professionals, parents, researchers, policymakers, and citizens) *need to do* regarding the issue. Authors will synthesize the literature and make recommendations for action.

I am proud that this book highlights the work of Bernice Lott and Heather Bullock. They draw together the psychology literature, their personal experiences, and their analyses of political and social realities to examine the topic of social class and economic injustice. Their work and their recommendations provide a superb example of using psychology to enhance the human condition and create a more just society.

Mary M. Brabeck, PhD
Book Series Editor
Steinhardt School, New York University

Psychology and Economic Injustice

1

Introduction

D espite the overwhelming evidence of its powerful contribution to human experience, social class remains a relatively neglected subject in psychology, including social psychology and feminist psychology. In this volume, we argue for increased empirical and theoretical attention to the antecedents and consequences of economic disparities, for greater understanding of the relationship between such disparities and gender, and for the need to apply our knowledge by proposing and supporting policies designed to ensure positive social change.

Throughout this book, we use the term *social class* to refer to positions within "the economic system of production, distribution, and consumption of goods and services in industrial societies" (Rothman, 2002, p. 6). Although *social class* and *socioeconomic status* are often used interchangeably in the psychological literature, *social class* is the more overtly political term that connotes differences in power. Socioeconomic status can be thought of as "a composite measure that typically incorporates economic status, measured by income; social status, measured by education; and work status, measured by occupation" (Dutton & Levine, as cited in Adler et al., 1994, p. 15). This does not make salient the intergroup dimensions of inequity that references to social class highlight. Social class, unlike socioeconomic status, focuses attention on socially constructed aspects of social standing, including differences in judgment and treatment of various classes.

In this chapter, we introduce the reader to what we see as critical issues facing low-income individuals and families, issues that have been ignored or not adequately addressed within psychology. These issues require research and call for activism and are areas in which psychologists and other social scientists could make significant contributions.

TOWARD A CLASS-INCLUSIVE FEMINIST PSYCHOLOGY

Feminist psychologists share with other feminist scholars some core assumptions and values (Lott, 1991) including (a) a recognition of the patriarchal nature of contemporary institutions and much of social life, (b) an understanding of the negative consequences of gender inequality, (c) a focus on the entire range of women's experiences and development, and (d) an activist orientation to social change in the interest of eliminating barriers to resources and thus eliminating power inequities. Such a perspective presents a clear imperative to situate women's lives in the context of their roles and social position and to examine the impact of ethnicity, sexual orientation, disability, and social class on lived experience. Within each of these categories, groups are distinguished from one another in terms of relative power, that is, in terms of access to the resources needed for a healthy, safe, and productive life.

Feminist psychologists share a growing recognition that the field requires maximum inclusion; that the social construct "woman" is not unitary and not simple; and that the experiences of those who are middle class, White, heterosexual, able-bodied, and living in the United States are not representative of the lives of other women (e.g., Hurtado, 1996). Simply adding or welcoming poor White women and women of color to a middle-class feminist movement is not the answer; rather, "the approach must be transformative, not additive" (Finn, 2002, p. 384). Hernandez and Leong (2004) reinforced this point by observing that many women of color do not call themselves feminists, despite agreeing with feminist goals, because they perceive the feminist movement as still focused on the concerns of middle-class White women. They argued persuasively that "feminism can't survive by helping women climb the corporate ladder while ignoring cuts to welfare. Family and medical leave only matter if we have jobs with benefits. Feminism has to recruit beyond college campuses" (p. 32).

Although there is ample documentation of the negative role played by patriarchal institutions and sexism in the lives of all women, the specific ways in which the greater power of men affects the lives of women are interwoven differently depending on myriad other factors. These factors can be loosely designated by the social categories of class, ethnicity, and so on. Both local and national politics still remain a sphere primarily for White men, and women who have made inroads and who wield some political influence are typically from privileged backgrounds with access to economic and social resources.

In this book, our emphasis is on a class-inclusive feminist psychology. Socioeconomic status influences the particular patriarchal institutions that must be grappled with and their effects. Consider what the institution of marriage typically or ideally means for a heterosexual middle-class woman in the United States. Her wedding is attended by 200 merrymaking guests at a party paid for by her parents. She has registered her gift preferences and will honeymoon at a beautiful vacation spot. The couple will return to jobs and the goal of purchasing a home in the not-too-distant future. Now consider what marriage might mean for a heterosexual low-income couple with fewer economic resources and lower paying job expectations and possibilities. There will be similarities in the attitudinal and behavioral correlates of being a wife or a husband for middle-class and working-class couples but significant differences as well (Lichter, Batson, & Brown, 2004; Wells & Baca Zinn, 2004). Unlike a low-income mother, one who is more affluent can look forward to respectful treatment in her children's schools (Lott, 2001), living in a neighborhood that is safe and attractive, shopping without food stamps, and perhaps buying occasional clothes in thrift stores because it is chic and not because it is necessary.

Although gender inequality has negative consequences for all women, these consequences are situated in class and ethnic contexts that determine their particular effects. It is no accident, for example, that HIV infection is rising steeply among poor Black women (Zierler & Krieger, 1998). A study that examined cases of AIDS contracted between 1982 and 1996 identified the huge national increase among Blacks, especially Black women, as powerfully accounted for by the increase in the percentage of Black male prisoners (cf. Morin, 2006).

Just as discussions of sexism and racism play a central role in feminist theory and practice, classism is also significant; it has been defined by Bullock (1995) as "the oppression of the poor through a network of everyday practices, attitudes, assumptions, behaviors, and institutional rules" (p. 119). *Institutional classism* refers to the maintenance of low status and barriers to resource access by social institutions, and *interpersonal classism* can be identified by the related but independent dimensions of *prejudice* (negative attitudes), *stereotypes* (beliefs), and *discrimination* (distancing or denigrating behavior).

Although psychologists "ostensibly honor equal opportunity . . . economic and political forces replicate and intensify longstanding structures of inequality whether measured in income distribution, educational opportunity, or social status" (Rosen, 1996, p. 337). As feminist psychology becomes increasingly sensitive to the ways in which economic injustice influences development and opportunities, choices, and necessities throughout the life span of girls and women, it must include discussions and analyses of social class and also of classism. Class, like gender, is descriptive of social category placement but also functions as a stimulus or cue for the covert and overt behavior of others. Feminist psychologists must make salient in their work as educators, scholars, and practitioners the multidimensional realities of social class in the United States.

CRITICAL ISSUES IN THE LIVES OF WORKING-CLASS WOMEN

Feminist scholarship, an integration of research and theory, has enriched the social sciences and humanities and has widened their scope. Within psychology, this has involved an insistence that researchers recognize the role played by sexist and racist assumptions in the development of their hypotheses and procedures. It has also resulted in an expansion of research areas to include a focus on the diversity of women's life experiences. This has led to the development of new research questions and the introduction of new concepts and issues (Lott, 1990, 1994, 1997; Unger, 1988). We can continue to widen our scope by giving serious consideration to the ways in which social class affects the lives of working-class women.

Social Class Identification

Some feminist writers, such as Walkerdine (1996), have begun to explore the question of why it seems "so difficult to get middle-class women to talk or write about their own lives as classed"(p. 356). Others have investigated the difficulties involved in openly discussing or revealing a working-class background (e.g., Reay, 1996). These writers have suggested that talking about social class makes people uncomfortable— perhaps because doing so implies that there are differences between classes that relate to inferiority–superiority, "deservingness," and assumptions about victims versus those with greater power. Walkerdine has argued that these feelings of discomfort involve an unwillingness to recognize how "one class comes to be responsible, often as professionals, for the moral regulation of the other" (Walkerdine, 1996, p. 357).

Social class identification is related to how social class positions are defined or understood. Ostrove and Cole (2003) have urged a "systematic research-based ... exploration of the *psychological* meaning of social class" (p. 680). Such a critical psychology of social class would not focus on class differences or the demographics of class but on understanding a person's position in a "classed location." Ostrove and Cole (2003) illustrated such an endeavor in a study of the meanings of social class in the context of higher education. An earlier project by A. J. Stewart and Ostrove (1993) explored the meaning of social class in women's lives as it relates to their sense of selfhood by studying the implications of class background for the experiences and development of a group of women students attending Radcliffe College in different time periods. It is not surprising that the authors reported experiences of alienation among the students with working-class backgrounds. Similar findings have been reported by Ritz (2003) in a study of low-income undergraduate students at two colleges in the Southeast.

More research and theoretical attention to the significance of social class on levels of personal feelings, perceptions, and social behavior are needed. There appears to be a lack of reality testing in the social class self-placement of many in the United States. For example, Moberg (2005) cited a recent *New York Times* poll in which 40% of the respondents said there was more chance today than 30 years ago of moving up in class status; 11% believed it was very likely they would become wealthy, and 34% believed it was somewhat likely. Moberg cited another poll, taken in 2000, that found that 39% thought they were in the wealthiest 1% of the population or soon would be.

Working for Wages, Not Salaries

Feminist psychologists have produced an extensive and important literature on careers and the effects of gender on relevant aspirations, preparations, attitudes, hiring discrimination, glass ceilings, and salary differentials. Much of this literature has limited relevance for girls whose final formal educational achievement may be a high school diploma or GED or for women who work in factories or as store clerks, waitresses, nurse's aides, or maids. There is a serious disconnect between the barriers and challenges faced by a college-educated, career-aspiring woman and her working-class counterpart. Bullock (2004) has examined class hierarchies within the workplace and how one's position reinforces status and provides information to others about one's power and authority.

Eisenstein (2005) presented a challenging argument that corporate and government policies to maximize profits have co-opted the aspect of feminism that focused on expanding women's role as paid workers in the labor force. She pointed out that the rapid rise in women's employment from 1970 to 2000 was accompanied by an enormous increase in the service sector, in which jobs more than doubled during that period, with 60% of the 53 million new jobs going to women. The proportion of adult women in the labor force has risen from 34% in 1960 to more than 60% today. As Eisenstein observed, "The idea that women, married or single, would spend most of their lifetime working outside the home had become normative" (p. 498). The service sector could provide jobs for women, but jobs with low wages, few if any benefits, and little opportunity for advancement or training.

In connection with the disconnect between career-focused research and working-class employment realities, such issues as union membership need to be considered. This subject is unlikely to be addressed in most books on the psychology of women, despite the fact that, as Finn (2002) noted, these are exciting new times for organized labor. Some authors such as Levi (2001) have urged unions to use their considerable "resources to combat persistent social and economic inequality" (p. 246). Should the Web site for working women within the AFL-CIO (http://www.unionvoice.org/aflcio_workingwomen/) be included as a resource for students? What is the experience of women in unions, in organizing, in leadership? What factors maintain patriarchy in such structures? The possible questions to be raised and answered are numerous, and middle-class feminists need to do the difficult work of stopping to consider what they do not know about the lives of their less affluent sisters. Many years ago, one of us attended a Society for the Psychology of Women (SPW) council meeting at a hotel in a large city. Attending this meeting required crossing a picket line because hotel workers were on strike.

When this subject was raised during the meeting, the response was one that made a deep impression in its relative lack of empathy or identification with or support for the strikers, reinforcing a disturbing conclusion about class bias.

R. M. Lee and Dean (2004) have pointed out that most Americans are working as skilled or unskilled laborers; that is, they are part of the working class. Government statistics document that 60% to 70% of U.S. workers are employed in working-class occupations, in "office support, construction, building maintenance, and sales" (R. M. Lee & Dean, 2004, p. 20). Despite the large numbers of such workers, the print media, in reports on the economy, emphasize news that centers on corporations and investments. A content analysis of articles printed in 1997 and 1998 in the *Los Angeles Times*, the largest newspaper in California (Kollmeyer, 2004), found few stories about the economic problems of workers. The newspaper "rarely used union leaders, workers, or their spokespersons as sources of information and viewpoints on the economy" (Kollmeyer, 2004, p. 449). The articles focused overwhelmingly on issues relevant to corporate interests.

The press rarely notes the dangers faced by those in low-income occupations in which there is a "higher risk of injury and death" (Bullock 2004, p. 231). Fligstein and Shin (2004), in reviewing changes in working conditions between 1976 and 2000, concluded that positive changes (e.g., in safety and physical surroundings) have occurred only in higher skilled, management, and professional occupations and that there has been a systematic erosion of conditions for lower skilled workers. Banks and Marshall (2005) have raised the question of the relationship between doing arduous labor and the resulting disabilities from such labor, which present greater barriers to those not able to purchase the health care and other services and goods needed to reduce the handicapping consequences.

At the beginning of 2005, the rate of participation in paid employment (the percentage of working-age adults with jobs or actively seeking them) was the lowest in 17 years at 65.8% (Aversa, 2005), and this unemployment problem was especially true for women. Economic problems continue to be particularly severe for single-mother families in which the woman heading the family is a low-wage worker (Kahne, 2004). In 2001, they numbered 13.1 million (almost 18% of all families in the United States). Unemployment is significantly greater than the national average for these workers, who have limited job skills and education. As Kahne (2004) noted, low-paid single mothers experience not only a "wage disadvantage relative to men in comparable jobs, but also . . . more frequent lay-offs, involuntary part-time work, job severance, and lack of health and pension benefits . . . [and] absence of child support" (p. 54). The poverty rate for single-mother families has steadily increased to a recent high of 35.5% (National Women's Law Center, personal communication, August 26, 2004).

War and Its Greater Demands on Working-Class Families

In the wars fought by the United States, it is the children of working-class families who have experienced most of the casualties and done most of the fighting and dying. For example, during the Vietnam War, 76% of soldiers were from working-class or low-income families (e.g., Halbfinger & Holmes, 2003). What social conditions currently motivate enlistment in the armed forces? What are the consequences for working-class women who give up their sons, and now their daughters as well, to war duty? How do middle-class women respond to this inequitable state of affairs?

Army recruiters understand social class very well, because they carefully target working-class high schools. A story in the *Boston Globe* about the strategies used in such schools reported that recruiters chaperone dances, and every prospective recruit "gets called at least six times" (Savage, 2004, ¶1). Recruiters distribute key chains and mugs in school cafeterias, follow students to sporting events and other places where they hang out (e.g., at malls and convenience stores), and offer job training and college scholarships. They offer sign-up bonuses of as much as $12,000 in cash and $70,000 in college aid. They "focus on the lower middle class in places with little economic opportunity" (Savage, 2004, ¶39). Halbfinger and Holmes (2003) interviewed members of the volunteer military and found that high on the list of reasons for joining was to gain a free college education, job skills, health coverage, and work experience. Minorities of color and recruits from low-income families are overrepresented in the military, whereas the middle class and wealthy are underrepresented. The researchers noted that more than 35% of enlisted women are Black.

Government Aid for Corporations Compared With That for Working Families

There are frequent news stories about welfare or entitlements, often accompanied by information about their costs, but one is less likely to read about corporate welfare. Thus, as the talk from Washington, DC, has centered on reductions in state block grant funds that help to finance Medicaid, child care, and other low-income assistance programs (Horney, Greenstein, & Kogan, 2005) and Congress has passed a bill to make it more difficult for families to declare bankruptcy when they are no longer able to pay their bills, corporations have been treated to one break after another. For example, 2005 was designated as a "tax holiday" year for American multinational corporations, during which they were permitted to bring "foreign profits back to the United States at a puny tax rate of 5.25 percent, compared with the normal corporate rate of 35 percent" ("Corporate Welfare Runs Amok," 2005 ¶1). It is ironic that this legislation was included in a bill called "The American Jobs Creation Act of 2004," because it was argued that the tax holiday would help release money for jobs. However, few of the uses approved for the repatriated funds were likely to create jobs. Instead, these funds were to be used for advertising, debt redemption, and payments for legal liabilities.

The contrast between federal legislative attention to the welfare of corporations and the affluent and to the welfare of working families is striking. This is abundantly clear from the results of a 2005 Harvard

University study cited by Jewell (2005) about the relationship between personal bankruptcy and costs associated with medical problems. About one half of all personal bankruptcies, according to the study, resulted from the inability to pay bills for costly illnesses that overwhelmed the financial resources of families, despite their having some form of medical insurance. The authors of the study estimated that about 2 million Americans are affected each year by "medical-caused bankruptcies" and that 87% of bankruptcies are related to medical problems, loss of a job, or dissolution of a marriage through divorce or separation (e.g., Eaton, 2005).

Given the social class position of most elected officials, it is not surprising that the needs of working families are not high among federal government priorities. What is disturbing is that feminists and women in positions of national leadership so often mirror this lack of concern. For example, the legislation that ended federal welfare and created a new program unfriendly to poor women (Temporary Assistance for Needy Families, discussed more fully in chap. 4) was supported by the majority of women in Congress. Among the 28 female Democrats in the House of Representatives at the time, 23, including the cochair and former cochair of the Women's Congressional Caucus, voted for the legislation (Eisenstein, 2005).

Zinn (2003) amply documented that "use of government for class politics to serve the needs of the wealthy and powerful, has continued throughout American history, down to the present day" (p. 684). On the basis of their own examination of financial disclosure information and reporting by a Capitol Hill newspaper, *Roll Call* (Keller, 2003), Lioz and Cassady (2003) found that 42% of U.S. senators and approximately 23% of U.S. representatives are millionaires compared with just 1% of the U.S. voting population. Political participation in the United States reflects the same inequalities as are present in education, occupation, and income, so that working-class interests are poorly represented in the political process and in government. Among a group of low-income adults interviewed in the South Bronx (Lawless & Fox, 2001), the central finding, that political activism is associated with material resources, was the same as that reported in studies with other populations. This phenomenon is of great and wide significance because, as Verba, Schlozman, and Brady (2004) pointed out, "the very inequality in political activity . . . militates against the implementation of policies designed to bring about greater educational, social, or economic equality" (p. 660).

The relative lack of political voice and influence by the working class is reflected in federal policies over the past 2 or 3 decades. Continued reductions in safety net programs such as welfare, food stamps, and unemployment insurance have been accompanied by a decrease in pensions and health care supports by business (Fligstein & Shin, 2004). The relationship between social class and the government is complex and circular. Structural inequities reduce political participation by those who lack the financial and social resources, as well as the necessary time and energy, to take part. This, in turn, helps to maintain the inequities because those who gain political power are those who already have greater access to resources and wish to maintain it. Those whose daily lives are most linked to government programs are least likely to engage in political activity and least likely to influence government policy (Lawless & Fox, 2001).

Reproductive Issues

The options for reproductive choice have long been fewer for less affluent women. Federal Medicaid funds are denied to them for abortions, and abortion services are more difficult to access. In 1976, Congress passed the Hyde Amendment, which prohibits the use of federal funds for abortions. State funds for abortions for poor women are available in only 15 states and the District of Columbia (Kennedy, 2001; Solinger, 2001). It can be argued that true reproductive freedom must include access to affordable health care (Hernandez & Leong, 2004). In addition, as new reproductive technologies have been developed, the gap between poor and more affluent women has widened even further. For example, the costs for in vitro fertilization procedures range from between $8,000 to $10,000 for a 2-week egg-retrieval cycle and $60,000 to $150,000 for a successful delivery. Clearly, as noted by Beckman and Harvey (2005), only the privileged few "can have access to many of these new options" (p. 2).

Social class is also salient when we examine technology involving the use of surrogate biological mothers to bear children for other women. Ciccarelli and Beckman (2005) studied the verbal self-reports of surrogate mothers that suggested that they choose to bear the children for altruistic reasons. Such responses, however, may be more socially approved than others that are not verbalized because, as the investigators noted, surrogate mothers generally have working-class backgrounds and their family incomes are modest.

Also relevant to reproductive choice are assumptions about what constitutes "correct" or "best" choices regarding motherhood. Finn (2002) argued that whereas prochoice advocates support contraception, pregnancy termination, and single motherhood, a poor woman having children is often judged negatively as "too young, too poor, too many," suggesting prochoice limits that mirror "contemporary Western middle-class notions of proper motherhood" (Finn, 2002, p. 390). These normative expectations are evident in the distribution of invasive contraceptives such as Norplant in low-income communities and the "illegitimacy reduction" bonuses received by states that decrease birth rates among unmarried welfare recipients without experiencing a corresponding increase in abortion rates (see Pierson-Balik, 2003).

Continued Stigmatization of the Poor

Although some evidence exists that media treatment of poverty and related issues such as homelessness has become more sympathetic in recent years (e.g., Bullock, Wyche, & Williams, 2001), the same conclusion cannot be reached about the professional social science literature. Buck, Toro, and Ramos (2005) conducted a content analysis of randomly selected journal articles dealing with homelessness that were published between 1974 and 2003. These data were compared with the results of an analysis of randomly selected articles from four major U.S. newspapers. In the professional literature, Buck et al. found that "deficits and deviant characteristics of homeless people were discussed to a significantly greater extent than the structural causes of homelessness over the entire 30-year time period" (p. 151). The investigators found that this was not true of the newspaper stories. Thus, pathology has remained a theme in how the psychological literature examines poverty (cf. Baker, 1996; Walkerdine, 1996) and welfare receipt (R. Lee & Curran, 2003).

The professional literature is consistent with attitudes toward the poor by the nonpoor, which continue to be more negative than those toward the middle class. The poor continue to be blamed for their poverty (e.g., Cozzarelli, Wilkinson, & Tagler, 2001). For example, a telephone interview study (Hunt, 2002) in Southern California of close to 3,000 respondents found that Protestants and Catholics were more likely than those with minority religious beliefs or nonaffiliates to agree with individualistic interpretations of poverty. That is, Protestants and Catholics were more likely to view poverty as the result of personal deficits. Another variable found to be related to stereotyped perceptions of welfare recipients is watching TV cable stations for news and entertainment (Sotirovic, 2001). More frequent use of this medium was associated with more negatively biased beliefs. Such findings point to the importance of challenging classist stereotypes (Lott, 2002a).

ADVOCACY FOR SOCIAL CHANGE

Publications and presentations from feminist perspectives typically include activist recommendations for achieving greater gender equity as well as equity for other groups with less access to resources (i.e., less power). Such a position follows from recognition of the negative consequences of patriarchy and sexism. Deriving prescriptions and proposals for positive social change from one's scholarship and practice is a natural progression from empirically obtained data. It is thus surprising to read the argument of Kitzinger and Wilkinson (2005) that "as psychologists, we do not have a lot to say about justice, rights, [and] . . . equality" (p. 186). They maintained that such concepts belong to other disciplines, like philosophy, political science, and law, and that psychologists "are confined to the discourse of mental health as a vehicle for pursuing social justice" (p. 186). This surprisingly narrow view of psychology neglects decades of research on the social (as well as personal) consequences of prejudice, discrimination, violence, justice-related behaviors, unsubstantiated beliefs, differential exposure to varied experiences, and so forth. The data psychologists gather on the effects of injustice and inequality on people's lives mandate that we not only share what we know but also propose remedies.

We agree with Frost and Oullette (2005) and Borshuk and Cherry (2005) that as psychologists, we can challenge with empirical data policies and ideologies built on unsubstantiated assumptions. Our tools permit us to scrutinize variables of significance in everyday life and intergroup relations and then suggest how what we know about social justice and injustice can be used to advance or improve human welfare. In so doing, we are not so much proposing revolutionary and untried policies and practices as we are building on a recognition of the social reality of our times. Jackson (2004) suggested that this was the significant role psychologists played in the Supreme Court's historic decision on *Brown v. Board of Education* (1954).

In this book, we give recognition to the social realities of economic inequities and injustice. Daily life for poor families is different in significant ways from what it is for middle-class families. From an ethnographic study focused on family life, Lareau (2003) observed that low-income mothers "scrimped to make food last until they were able to buy more, waited for buses that didn't come, [and] carried children's laundry out to public washers" (p. 35). Interviews with poor mothers and their teenage children (Kurz, 2002) also have highlighted the special difficulties and challenges faced daily in keeping children safe and in school while living in dangerous environments with few resources. A tragic reality for so many mothers in these environments is the constant threat of violence. There is heartbreaking truth in these words by Herbert (2005): "Burying the young has long since become routine in poor black and Latino neighborhoods" (¶3). Can middle-class women even imagine what it is like to face the threat of community violence on a daily basis and the consequences of grieving for children, friends, partners, and family members (Jenkins, 2002)?

We are urging more serious attention to such realities by psychologist educators, researchers, and practitioners, particularly from within feminist perspectives. Feminism has already enriched our discipline by raising new empirical and methodological questions and proposing new theoretical concepts and approaches. Economic justice as a differential reality in the lives of women demands full inclusion in our work.

ENLARGING PSYCHOLOGY'S FOCUS

It is not at all accidental that a *Resolution on Poverty and Socioeconomic Status*, adopted by the Council of Representatives of the American Psychological Association (APA, 2000), was the direct result of the work of the Task Force on Women, Poverty, and Public Assistance established by SPW. One of the goals of the task force was to bring such a resolution to APA. To this end, members of the task force worked with APA's Committee on Urban Initiatives, directed by Leslie Cameron. This committee took on the responsibility of drafting the formal resolution and presenting substantial evidence from a wide variety of sources to support recommendations for research, education, and practice. The APA resolution (see the Appendix) was preceded by two widely disseminated reports prepared by the SPW task force, one entitled *Implementing Welfare Policy to Insure Long-Term Independence and Well-Being* (APA, Division 35, 1997) and the other, *Making "Welfare to Work" Really Work* (APA, Division 35 Task Force on Women, Poverty, and Public Assistance, 1998). The latter report, requested by and sent to members of the U.S. Congress and a large number of agencies and individuals, presented myths and facts about welfare and information and recommendations on domestic violence, education and training, work structure and benefits, child care, and health care. The first words of the document came right to the point in asserting that "welfare is not the problem—poverty is the problem" (p. 1). Another accomplishment of the SPW task force was the publication of a *Journal of Social Issues* volume (Lott & Bullock, 2001), "Listening to the Voices of Poor Women."

The work of the task force, the membership of which changed during its 4-year existence, made a difference. For SPW, establishment of the task force marked the formal recognition of the relationship between gender, social class, and poverty. For APA, the work of the task force resulted in acceptance of the importance of social class as a variable in human behavior. We honor the contributions made by all the members of the first and second SPW task forces, some of whom participated as graduate students: Diane Bowker-Turner, Anne Brodsky, Catherine Cozzarelli, Katherine Gamble, Ingrid Johnston-Robledo, Donna McDonald, Guerda Nicolas, Pamela Reid, Stephanie Riger, Joy Rice, Joan Rollins, Lenore Rubin, Janis Sanchez-Hucles, Renee Saris, Jacqueline Scarbrough, Hazel Spears, and Karen Wyche. The authors of this volume were also members of both task forces. Recognition of the power of social class in everyday life continues within APA, as indicated by the establishment in February 2005 of its own new 2-year Task Force on Socioeconomic Status.

ORGANIZATION OF THIS BOOK

Personal reflections by each of the authors follow this chapter. Our reflections are presented as illustrations of critical class scholarship. We discuss our class history and our paths to feminism and class consciousness, attending specifically to the impact of gender, class, and ethnicity on our personal experiences and our professional and political lives. We attempt to trace relationships among personal experiences and development as feminist social psychologists and researcher–activists committed to social justice.

From our personal narratives we move to a chapter in which we review the scope and consequences of institutional classism. Discussed and analyzed are the resources required for human welfare (health care, nutrition, education, child care, adequate income, and housing), and systemic barriers to accessing these resources are documented. Particular attention is paid to how low-income women and their families in the United States are systematically impeded in their efforts to reach "good life" goals. Multiple sources of information about economic inequality are presented, including data from psychological research and other social science disciplines, national statistics, and reports by journalists. We follow this chapter with one that focuses on the use of classist–racist–sexist framing by the media and government to mobilize support for disparity-enhancing policies (e.g., welfare reform, dividend tax elimination). The political rhetoric of legislative initiatives to benefit the richest segments of the U.S. population is deconstructed, revealing covert and overt bias. Accusations of "class warfare" are examined to understand how they are used to silence opposition to policies that benefit the wealthy and how they are related to dominant beliefs about individualism and meritocracy.

The final chapter in this book presents recommendations for policy. We outline areas in which clear, concrete, and important steps can be taken to advocate for social justice on the basis of empirical knowledge and feminist values. We present recommendations for promoting economic justice in the public sphere and argue that federal and state governments must move from punitive "personal responsibility" models to more generous and comprehensive models that promote human welfare. We take seriously the question asked by Fine (2002), "Who is absent, who is excluded, and who is refused an audience?" (p. 20), and suggest ways to end the exclusion of poor women and their families from decision making and from the attention of our discipline. We propose a research and advocacy agenda for psychology and feminist psychology that will advance social justice.

2

Growing Up Poor *and* Middle Class: Heather Bullock's Story

When I teach my course, "The Social Psychology of Poverty and Social Class," students are surprised to learn that my family was solidly middle class during most of my childhood but that we were also on welfare and were intermittently homeless during my high school years. This simply isn't the class background expected or imagined for a White university professor, and there is little about my life today to hint at these former economic hardships. Yet, it is estimated that 51.1% of people in the United States experience at least 1 year of poverty during their lives and nearly two thirds of Americans will reside in a household that at some point receives some form of "welfare" (e.g., food stamps, cash assistance, Medicaid; Rank & Hirschl, 2001, 2002). The myth remains that "nice middle-class families" don't need to worry about poverty and that financial insecurity is a reflection of personal failure. This myth in part results from a strong taboo against openly discussing the real vulnerability of most Americans to becoming poor, particularly those who work hard in low-paying, dead-end jobs. We are taught to believe that middle class is the norm and that discussing one's real financial status is inappropriate (Baker, 1996; Mantsios, 2004).

Some feminist scholars have sought to make poverty and privilege "visible" by deconstructing the social meanings of race, ethnicity, class, and gender (Bettie, 2000; Fine & Weis, 1998) and by uncovering and challenging the methods by which power and access to resources are distributed. Narrative and other reflective analyses of the intersections of class, gender, race, and ethnicity have played a particularly crucial role in transforming understanding of identity formation, pathways to critical resistance, the individual and social costs of prejudice, the interpersonal dynamics of power relations, and the relationship between the personal and political (Adair, 2002; Cohen, 1998; Phoenix & Tizard, 1996; Russell, 1996; Weis, 2003). These narratives assure those of us who live or have lived at the margins that we are not alone.

I share my own story of personal and political nexus in appreciation of the advocacy, scholarship, and wisdom of feminists who have made finding my own voice that much easier. Attending college in the mid-1980s and graduate school in the early 1990s, I reaped the benefits of the feminist movement and progressive scholarship. In college I took courses on the psychology of gender and in graduate school had the privilege of working with strong feminist psychologists and scholars in other disciplines, but the path I followed still had its share of twists and turns, and class, gender, and race have influenced both my life and my life chances.

GROWING UP MIDDLE CLASS AND POOR

I was born in 1966 in Tarrytown, New York, to White, college-educated parents. My father was a moderately successful real estate lawyer in New York City and a justice of the peace in our town. My mother, who was a social worker before she married, chose to be a full-time homemaker after she married. After having three sons, my mother did not plan to have another child, but when she became pregnant in her late 30s, a full 10 years after the birth of my youngest brother, she decided to follow the pregnancy to term despite the medical advice of the day. As the youngest and the only daughter, my birth was a celebrated event.

My early childhood was economically secure. We owned a relatively large home, installed an above-ground pool in our backyard, took summer vacations at a resort in Maine, and enjoyed lavish Christmas holidays. My mother dedicated considerable energy to encouraging my "femininity"; she cared greatly about my physical appearance, setting my long hair on rollers each night before bed and insisting that I wear dresses. I enjoyed my mother's attention and wanted to please her, even though my brothers teased me about being a "girly-girl."

Our family may have appeared happy, but my early years were, in fact, tumultuous. My mother was depressed and an alcohol abuser, a problem that my father avoided by working late. Unlike my brothers, who could come and go as they pleased, I couldn't escape my mother's drinking and anger. I was a well-liked but quiet child who used books to get away from the problems at home. I was an avid reader throughout my childhood.

When my father was home, my parents fought bitterly about everything, including our finances, which made me conscious of money at a very young age. Expenses always seemed to outpace resources, and even when our family was relatively comfortable, money was still a source of considerable anxiety. My mother equated earning power with "masculinity" and derided my father for not commanding a higher salary. My father tried to avoid being drawn into these dead-end arguments, particularly when my mother had been drinking, but rarely succeeded in doing so.

During this time, one of my brothers, who still lived at home, developed a serious drug problem, which further contributed to an already fraught environment. Because my brother's drug use was public, there was concern that he would be arrested and embarrass my father, who at that time held a position as town judge. Despite the unrest in my home life, I don't remember anyone trying to intervene or any expression of public concern about our situation. Years later when I was in high school and my family was poor, I learned that the privacy given to my family earlier is only afforded to those who are middle class.

When I was in third grade, my father took a new position as a lawyer with a small corporation that developed shopping malls. With two of my brothers away at college, I moved to a small fishing and resort town in Massachusetts with my parents. I loved my new home and its beautiful beaches, but the transition to a new school was difficult for me. I was shy, and my math skills trailed behind those of my new peers. It took some time for me to make new friends and adjust to the schoolwork. Having left a school in New York that was struggling with racial desegregation and rioting, the curriculum in my new predomi-nantly White, middle-class school was considerably more advanced. Although some of my classmates were Cape Verdean, most were Irish Catholic.

Shortly after our arrival in Massachusetts, my brother's drug problem resulted in his arrest in New York for possession with intent to sell. As a courtesy to my father, the police waited to arrest my brother until we left the state. My father's respected community status prevented my brother from serving prison time (this is a class and race privilege that is reflected in differential arrest and incarceration rates; see Myers, 1987).

In the late 1970s, the corporation that my father worked for went bankrupt, and with limited savings, we fell on hard times. My father, then in his 50s and without a professional network in our new state, remained underemployed, earning money only through part-time work. When I was in sixth grade, my family received food stamps and I qualified for "free lunch," an incredibly shameful experience. My lunch card was visibly different from the ones used by classmates who paid for their lunches. To avoid being seen using my card, I went to the back of the lunch line, and if anyone stood behind me, I would create a reason to "lose" my spot. I also stopped going to the supermarket because I didn't want to be seen with my parents when they paid with food stamps. If they were embarrassed by our situation, they never discussed it with me, although my mother blamed my father and derided his ability to provide for us financially. I did not question why my mother did not look for paid work.

Toward the end of my 1st year of high school, my parent's financial situation finally bottomed out. The county sheriff served us with eviction papers, and we lost our home to the mortgage company. My mother, who took great pride in our home and her skill as a decorator, was devastated. My father stoically reassured us that we would be fine, but I was afraid that I would be separated from my parents. As our finances had worsened, our family had come under closer public scrutiny. Earlier in the year, my mother had been hospitalized for alcohol-related problems, and I had been scheduled for weekly appointments with the school social worker. I became increasingly conscious of the public dimensions of our family issues and worried that the social worker might have the authority to declare my family "unfit" to care for me.

Once we were evicted from our home, our situation became truly desperate. Our suburban town had few apartments, and my parents did not want to move out of town. We could not qualify for those apartments in any case. Like many people who suddenly find themselves in dire financial straits, we did not have the money for the required deposit equal to the first and last months of rent. Our difficulties were compounded by the approaching tourist season and sky-high rental prices. So we moved to the one place that did not require such a lump sum—a local motel.

It is erroneously believed that people who live in motels are wasting money out of stupidity or because they are engaged in illegal activities that require moving around to avoid being caught. This is rarely true. People who believe this probably cannot imagine how difficult it is to find the money for a 2-month deposit or have possibly suppressed their own early experiences with this kind of struggle.

Before moving into the motel, we sold most of our furniture at a yard sale, but we still did not have enough money for the apartment deposit. The motel room we ended up in was at the beach. There was nothing glamorous about our living conditions, although I tried to portray "our move to the beach" as such to my classmates, because school was still in session when we were evicted from our house. With only a miniature refrigerator and hot plate to prepare food, we didn't have much to eat. Because the three of us lived in one room, we had little privacy.

After a month, my parents told me I could no longer stay with them, and I moved in with the family of one of my closest friends. I appreciated my hosts' generosity, but I sensed their pity. My friends' families never overtly criticized my parents, but I felt that they judged them in pejorative terms and, by default, extended that judgment to me. My parents did not have a phone in their room but drove over weekly to visit. Despite the tension during these visits, I missed my parents greatly when they went back to their motel room. After 5 months, we moved into a furnished rental home at the start of my sophomore year. We repeated this cycle annually—moving into a new rental at the start of the school year and separating in the summer when I returned to friends' homes and my parents moved to different local motels.

Despite this "different" life, my interests were like those of many White, middle-class, heterosexual, adolescent girls; I was more concerned with dating and having the right clothes than with my schoolwork (Galambos, Almeida, & Petersen, 1990; Orenstein, 1994). As a member of a popular clique, an active social life diverted my attention from my family's financial problems. I had a couple of serious boyfriends, but my girlfriends provided my emotional support.

I was able to keep up with my middle-class friends through the money I earned by working as a babysitter, a cashier at a local movie theatre, and later as a waitress at a seasonal "clam shack." Once I was old enough to be employed, my parents urged me to work as many hours as the law allowed, and I hoped that by having the right things I could disguise my family's poverty (Nenga, 2003). By senior year, I spent more hours in paid employment than in the classroom, leaving school early to earn course credit for my work as a waitress. I did not think about the schoolwork I was missing, nor did I understand that this option was common among low-income students.

I was not particularly interested in going to college and felt that I was earning good money as a waitress. Because most of my immediate family had earned bachelor's degrees, however, it was assumed that I would go to college. Through Pell grants, scholarships, student loans, and the work-study program, I was able to attend the same small liberal arts college that my parents and youngest brother had graduated from. Like many teenagers, I was unaware at the time of the advantages going to college would provide in my future. Had my parents not insisted and had there not been a culture of going to college in my family, I would have continued waitressing. I rationalized giving in to the push to go to college by regarding it as a chance to leave my family's financial and other problems behind and to become a "new person." I had no idea what a powerful experience college would be or how much my economic prospects would improve because of it.

DEVELOPING FEMINIST AND CLASS CONSCIOUSNESS

I wanted to become a social worker like my mother, but as is true of many young women, I did not have a realistic understanding of different career paths (Sidel, 1990). This disconnect was evident in my dream of becoming a social worker *and* living in a penthouse apartment overlooking Boston Harbor with my girlfriends. My first course in social psychology helped ground my interests; it examined gender roles, and I resonated with the content. I was excited to see connections between academic work and real-world problems and felt validated by research that paralleled my own beliefs and experiences (Liss, O'Connor, Morosky, & Crawford, 2001; Macalister, 1999; Worell, Stilwell, Oakley, & Robinson, 1999).

My interest in gender issues was fueled by the sexism and emphasis on appearance that pervaded my small, rural campus. Women's status was determined by their desirability to men, and individuals and sororities were ranked by physical attractiveness. It was the mid-1980s and, with the fitness craze in full force, thinness defined beauty. Eating disorders were common, and in a dorm room next to the showers, over the sounds of running water, I listened to women purge. The Greek system dominated social life, and although I wanted the ready-made network of friends I would gain, I decided not to join a sorority after attending a pledge meeting and feeling that the sisters were more interested in the man I was dating than in me.

My mixed-class background, a significant source of discomfort during my college years, also deepened my commitment to feminism. My closest friends were from working-class backgrounds, but interactions with peers who were from wealthy families underscored how different our experiences were. During the summers, they traveled to Europe or spent time at their vacation homes, while I worked 60 to 70 hours per week as a waitress and restaurant manager. Until that time, I had thought of class primarily in terms of material goods (i.e., owning a home or a car), but I began to understand economic privilege as access to the resources that are important for physical, social, mental, and emotional welfare and that provide freedom of choice in many arenas of life.

There was no doubt that compared with some of my peers, I was disadvantaged, but as a college student, I also recognized my relative advantage. A bitter town–gown divide pervaded the region, and my work-study job at the local United Way office exposed me to the consequences of deindustrialization. With local businesses languishing, I distributed heating vouchers and packages of food to low-income families. Even though I had been on the receiving end of such services, I was unprepared for the frustration, embarrassment, despair, and gratitude that recipients would express and the helplessness I would feel to change their situation.

When I entered the University of Rhode Island's experimental social psychology program as a graduate student in the fall semester of 1988, I planned to study sexism in the workplace. As a female restaurant manager, my authority had been called into question frequently, and I was eager to document the double standard of perceiving agentic men as strong but agentic women as aggressive (Carli, 2001; Schein, 1975). My master's thesis examined gendered evaluations of managers, but my interests shifted when I took a seminar on the social psychology of poverty, a course that I can truly say changed my life. My psychology training had focused on gender, race, and ethnicity, not on class or classism (Reid, 1993; Saris & Johnston-Robledo, 2000). This was my first academic exposure to the social psychological dimensions of economic (in)justice, and I wanted to learn as much as I could about women's poverty and the U.S. welfare system. I began attending welfare rights meetings at the George Wiley Center in Providence, Rhode Island. It was an exciting time, because I found that I could do good research on personally and politically meaningful issues. My doctoral project compared middle-class and welfare-recipient attributions for poverty and attitudes toward welfare reform (Bullock, 1999). Interpersonal and institutional classism, welfare policy, and class-based political mobilization, interests that I developed as a graduate student, remain my primary interests today.

MOVING BETWEEN DIFFERENT WORLDS

My first academic position was at a small liberal arts college in the Midwest in 1995. An old-boy network pervaded the college, and some of my colleagues were paternalistic. Each summer a group of powerful male faculty went white-water rafting, and although visiting male professors were sometimes invited, female faculty never were. Weekly basketball games also excluded female professors. As an untenured assistant professor under the age of 30, directly challenging these norms was difficult, but I was part of a small but strong feminist community, and we created an alternative network.

When I took the job, my partner had needed another year to complete his doctoral work, so I moved to the Midwest without him. When he joined me a year later, he had completed his doctorate in social psychology. We struggled to find a full-time academic position for him. My department was unmoved by our plight until I was offered a position at another college; to encourage me to stay they offered him a visiting professorship.

In addition to these professional struggles, I worried about being so far from my parents, who were then living in an apartment in Fall River, Massachusetts. Although they were no longer in immediate danger of homelessness, they lived month to month without significant savings. Both had numerous medical problems and, like 45.8 million other Americans, no health insurance (U.S. Census Bureau, 2005). Each week my mother visited an oncology clinic for checkups, chemotherapy, and blood transfusions. Her expenses were covered by a state program, which provided assistance to the working poor, and later by Medicaid.

Although a heavy teaching load made pursuing my research interests difficult, after the passage of the Personal Responsibility and Work Opportunity Reconciliation Act (P.L. 104-193) I continued studying the relationship between attributions for poverty, classist stereotypes, and support for welfare policy. I also collaborated with a local community action group, and together we designed a program to raise awareness of poverty and reduce classist stereotypes on college campuses.

I found this work rewarding but wanted to be engaged in efforts directed toward broader social change. In the fall of 1998, I left my teaching job to spend a year in Washington, DC, as an American Psychological Association Congressional Fellow in the Democratic Committee Office on Health, Education, Labor, and Pensions under the direction of Senator Edward Kennedy. As a legislative aide, I worked on a wide range of issues, including welfare policy, food stamp policy, early childhood education, and youth violence. It was an exhilarating experience and a chance to learn about the legislative process and the role of social science research in decision making.

In the fall of 1999, I returned to academia as an assistant professor at the University of California at Santa Cruz. The social psychology program's justice orientation and the university's support for feminist scholarship made this an ideal position. When I accepted this job, I was careful to look into the university's treatment of female faculty. Although women and minorities are underrepresented at the highest levels of the professorate, Santa Cruz is among the more diverse University of California campuses, with women and ethnic minorities making up approximately 36% and 25% of the faculty, respectively (Academic Human Resources, 2004). Despite these strengths, it is a difficult place for dual-career couples. After a year of underemployment, however, my partner obtained a research-oriented position in the campus administration, and in 2003 I was granted tenure.

When I speak with low-income women or spend time with my less financially secure family members, I am conscious of moving between "different worlds" and of the privileges that I enjoy as a White, middle-class professional. My brother beat his drug problem, but with an arrest record and no college degree, his job options are limited (Egan, 2005). He worked at a mattress factory for many years and was able to support his family. However, since the plant closed, he has moved around to different discount chains, and his family has experienced several periods of homelessness. My father, as he aged, also remained poor, but his situation became more secure. He lived in two nursing homes, first in Massachusetts with my mother and, after her death in 2002, in California near me. With no property or assets, Medicaid covered his medical expenses but his "free" care came at high cost. Low-income California patients in long-term care may keep only $35 per month of their Social Security check for expenses and must use the remainder to pay for their care.

Caregiving, whether for children or the elderly, continues to be women's work (Himmelweit, 1999), and as the only daughter, arranging my parents' housing, medical care, and social services fell exclusively on my shoulders. It is difficult, invisible work, and I worried about the quality of my father's care until his death in 2005. Once, during a 2:00 a.m. emergency room visit, a doctor, after reviewing my father's insurance information, wanted to transfer him to another hospital. Although discrimination was rarely this overt, I worried about the medical choices made on his behalf that I may not have been privy to. I am also troubled by the institutional racism, sexism, and classism that made it possible to pay poverty-level wages to the Latina aides who cared for him.

My teaching and research focus broadly on the social psychological dimensions of economic injustice. Over the past 10 years, I have investigated how different socioeconomic groups perceive poverty and justify their class status relative to others (Bullock & Limbert, 2003; Bullock & Waugh, 2005). Examining relationships among classist stereotypes, attributions for poverty, and support for antipoverty and welfare policies is a central dimension of this research (Bullock, Williams, & Limbert, 2003). I am also working to document poor women's experiences of interpersonal and institutional classism. As of this writing, I am studying the personal (e.g., attributions for poverty and wealth; beliefs about upward mobility) and situational (e.g., discrimination, termination of benefits) factors that contribute to low-income women's political mobilization. The overarching goals of these projects are to create spaces for the voices of low-income women to be heard and to dismantle interpersonal and institutional classism in the field of psychology and in society.

These would be impossibly lofty goals without the dedication, ingenuity, and persistence of a vast network of feminist activists and scholars, past, present, and future. Economic inequality is among our most pressing social problems. Reducing classist bias presents significant challenges, but as our foremothers have demonstrated, a more just society is not only possible, it is worth fighting for.

3

Working-Class Origins and Class-Conscious Awakening: Bernice Lott's Story

I was born in 1930, the third living child and the third daughter of immigrant parents living among other Jewish, Italian, and Irish working-class families in Brooklyn, New York. My mother had come from a shtetl in Eastern Europe (Russian Poland), much like the one depicted in *Fiddler on the Roof.* She never went to school and came to this country by herself in steerage when she was 14. Because children under 16 were not permitted into the United States without an accompanying adult, she claimed to be 2 years older than she was. I now take some pride in telling those who complain about illegal immigrants that my mother had lied to enter this country. She boarded in an aunt's house on the East Side of Manhattan until she married my father at the age of 20. Like so many other Jewish immigrants, she worked in the garment industry, in the sweatshops. She boasted to me that she was called "Red Annie" when the workers went on strike. She never learned

Some of the material in this chapter originally appeared in the chapter "Who Ever Thought I'd Grow Up to Be a Feminist Foremother?" by B. Lott, in *Feminist Foremothers in Women's Studies, Psychology, and Mental Health* (pp. 309–323), by P. Chesler, E. D. Rothblum, and E. Cole (Eds.), 1995, New York: Haworth.

to read or write in any language, but my clever mother somehow devised ways to get off at the correct subway stops when she shepherded her children to doctors, clinics, and shops.

My mother's life was difficult, like that of many immigrant Jewish women (Davidman & Tenenbaum, 1994; Kramer & Masur, 1976; Siegel & Cole, 1997), but we children were always well fed and well dressed. Her greatest pleasure came from our appearance and accomplishments. She was a champion bargain hunter, and she pocketed every lost coin she found on the city streets. When there was a brief respite from keeping house and shopping for food at the best prices, she sang Yiddish folk songs to me, told me stories about the old country, and let me play with her treasured scarves and bridal veil.

My father's background was quite different. He had been to gymnasium (high school) in a fairly large Polish city then part of the Austro-Hungarian Empire. He was the son of restaurant owners who tearfully let him go off as a teenager with a stranger on a journey to the United States. My father proudly spoke many languages and was an avid reader of Yiddish fiction and newspapers. He was a lover of song, dance, and good times, and he was also a hard worker, a skilled umbrella maker, and a waiter, often working two jobs. Just after I was born, he landed a full-time job as a clerk at the Brooklyn Navy Yard, a job he kept until retirement. He supplemented a meager (but steady) salary with income from other jobs that included, for many years, the selling of knishes from a pushcart. At work he was known as "the Reverend," because he led Jewish services during holiday times. He had served in the U.S. Army during World War I and was a strong patriot, frequently at odds with his daughters about politics.

During the 19 years I lived at home with my family, we moved from one rundown neighborhood to another, searching for something better or cheaper. My mother was always on the lookout for newly painted apartments that came with the first month's rent thrown in as an inducement. After I left home, my parents moved into subsidized low-income housing projects—dismal looking and poorly maintained.

My parents fought with each other loudly and abusively, and my two older sisters were more actively involved in the outside world than in their family. When I was 8 and my mother 38, she gave birth to a fourth child, my brother. This immediately changed my status from that of baby sister to big sister; thus, I have been both the youngest and the oldest in my family. In addition to taking on responsibilities for the care of my brother, I took on the role of parental go-between and peacemaker.

My greatest joys growing up were going to the library, going on school trips to museums, going to Manhattan on the subway to window-shop and people-watch, going to the movies, and eating Chinese food with friends for a Sunday lunch. I was a voracious reader—from Nancy Drew mysteries and Gothic romances to the complete works of Charles Dickens; these had been collected by my mother from stamps given by the life insurance salesman for premiums paid on time. I also loved going to the Yiddish theater with my parents on the rare occasions when they could be in each other's company peacefully.

At school, I was encouraged by some teachers who were not put off by the fact that my mother spoke with an accent, never participated in parents' activities, and practically never set foot in school except to bring me lunch on rainy days. We were a low-income, immigrant Jewish family, and I can empathize now with my mother's embarrassment about her status as outsider and her inability to read. Fathers, in those days, were not expected to come to school, which was just as well, because my father's involvement in my life was minimal beyond the occasions when he took me to movies. But school, even with the frequent changes caused by our many moves, was fun and easy—I skipped second (or third) and eighth grades—and offered me a sanctuary from the tense atmosphere at home.

I knew that my family did not live like the people in the movies, but neither did many others I knew. Yet, some episodes stand out sharply for me as clear markers of low-income life. I can still feel the frustration my mother and I encountered in health clinics, where we often waited for hours for attention from overworked and sometimes grumpy medical personnel. And one year, in elementary school, I was found to have nits (lice eggs) in my hair; the treatment was kerosene shampoos and fine-tooth combing. For years I was in dread each time my class had to line up to have our hair examined with a gingerly held pencil by a grim-faced teacher or nurse. Similar demeaning experiences were shared by others like me. For example, Adair (2002) remembered that in yearly medical checkups, "the school nurse sucked air through her teeth as she donned surgical gloves to check only the hair of poor children for lice" (p. 457).

When I got to my second junior high school, social class became sharply discernible to me. This phenomenon of "class differences ... noticed for the first time" in school (Ostrove & Cole, 2003, p. 684) has been discussed by others (e.g., Adair, 2002; Dodson, 1998; Schein, 1995). In my case, my family had moved into a more middle-class area when one of my sisters was able to contribute to the family income. We even got our first telephone! At my new school there were clear differences among the students in how they dressed and where they lived. A new friend who wore wool plaid skirts and cashmere sweaters invited me to go home with her after school—on a bus. Because I walked to school, this was exciting. I remember her nicely furnished house and the milk and cookies. I also remember never being invited again and what must have been the beginning of my class consciousness. I imagined that my classmate's mother, who had been at home, had not approved of me—perhaps because of my clothes, my conversation, or the neighborhood in which I lived. What pleasure I felt when I moved ahead of this girl in a spelling bee!

POLITICAL AND INTELLECTUAL AWAKENINGS

A major consequence of realizing that I was not a welcome part of the plaid skirt and sweater set group was that I moved toward friendship with other working-class girls and to urban street life. I learned how to filch things from Woolworth's, where luckily I escaped detection, and

I still experience anxiety in the presence of police, recalling scenes of neighborhood kids being spread-eagled and searched.

When it was time for high school, I chose to go with my friends to a working-class technical school for girls that specialized in commercial subjects and art instead of to the more prestigious multicurriculum coed school in my district. At the time, I did not fully understand the class implications of this choice, but I must have felt that I would be more comfortable among my own working-class girlfriends than in the school that most high schoolers in my neighborhood attended. Because neither of my school's special curricula had any interest for me, however, I chose an optional academic track, taking 4 years of science and mathematics. I assisted in the biology lab and got deeply involved in dramatics and politics. I do not know how I would have fared in a larger school competing with boys and worrying about clothes, hair, and dates, but I suspect that the outcome for me might have been very different.

In high school, I slowly drifted away from my old friends. I was one of a few non-Black students who belonged to the Frederick Douglass Club. We often sat at an ethnically diverse lunch table. I got into serious trouble once when my homeroom teacher observed one morning that my attention was on a book instead of on her reading from the New Testament. Her report of my "bad character" led to a semester's delay in my election to an honor society for which my good grades had made me eligible, but at graduation I received both the science and drama medals.

When my income-sharing sister left to go to college out of state, my family had to move back to the low-income neighborhood from which we had come. During all of my high school years, and then 3 years of commuter college, we lived across the street from shops and open pushcarts or stalls selling everything from live chickens to fruits and vegetables to pickles in brine-filled wooden barrels. The reaction to this neighborhood, during my 1st year in college, by a young man I was crazy about contributed to another significant rise in my class consciousness. He was older, a sophomore, and a veteran of World War

II; we had met at a summer camp where we both worked (he as a photography counselor and I as a waitress). One afternoon he walked home with me to my family's superclean but shabby and dreary apartment above a beauty shop and a delicatessen, on a street lined with pushcarts and vendors. Our relationship never moved forward after that. We were from starkly different neighborhoods and different social classes, and I could sense his discomfort.

Despite my academic achievements in high school, no counselor encouraged me to apply for a scholarship at a private college. It must have been assumed that someone in my economic situation had only one option—a free education at one of the New York City colleges. One older sister was attending a private university with the help of her veteran husband's GI bill stipend, and another sister had gone to Brooklyn College, but I remember being tempted to forgo college for the life of a secretary or bookkeeper (jobs I had done during summer vacations). I was persuaded to take the entrance examination for Brooklyn College and passed it. The year was 1946, veterans were returning from World War II, and New York's city colleges were using a higher entrance exam score for women than for men (not just for veterans). I suppose this was my first clear introduction to sexism.

Brooklyn College was wonderful, filled with bright and articulate students and challenging teachers. It took just one course in psychology to show me where I belonged. It was a joy to discover that there were methods by which I could test answers to questions about human social behavior. And so a social psychologist was born.

A few fine women professors were important models for me as an undergraduate, but we had no contact outside of class. I worked 10 hours a week at a college office, and because I had no money to spend on textbooks, I did all of my reading and studying in the library. The need to take careful and detailed notes became a skill that has served me well ever since. I also spent many hours in political activity both on and off the campus. I got into trouble when a group I was part of organized a rally and march to protest the dean's canceling of a talk by a radical speaker we had invited. This resulted in censure, and a letter to that effect was placed in my student records folder.

"GROWING UP" AND EXPERIENCING GENDER IN MARRIAGE AND GRADUATE SCHOOL

At the end of my junior year, at the age of 19, I left college to get married to a fellow psychology student and campus activist, a war veteran, 6 years older than I was, who had been accepted for graduate school at the University of California, Los Angeles (UCLA). We took a 5-day coach train trip across the country. It was not until a year later that I took my first airplane flight on what in those days was called a "nonscheduled" cross-country flight on a two-engine propeller plane— a trip that took 21 hours.

I was not able to enter UCLA immediately, so I worked full-time for a Christmas tree company until spring semester 1950. After admission, I completed my undergraduate work in two semesters, then passed an entrance exam for the graduate program in psychology, and began work toward a doctoral degree. My education at UCLA would not have been possible without the GI Bill, which paid my husband's tuition, provided him with a financial stipend, and made us eligible for low-cost veterans' student housing. I covered our other expenses with scholarships and part-time jobs, and the good state of California let me pay in-state tuition. My jobs included working for an accounting firm in Beverly Hills that handled the finances of Hollywood stars; working as an office assistant in the College of Nursing; and later, working as a research assistant with my major professor.

Women students were a tiny minority in my graduate program. The dean of the college (who was also the department head) greeted me on my first day and told me that although my credentials were excellent, he knew that training me would be a waste of everyone's time and energy because I would undoubtedly get pregnant and leave the field. Sandra Scarr (1987) has related an almost identical incident; when she was interviewed for admission to Harvard's graduate program in 1960, Gordon Allport told her, "We hate accepting women here" (p. 26). Perhaps the words I heard on my first day as a graduate student served as a challenge. I certainly never forgot them, nor the fact that two of the other graduate women in my department attempted suicide; one was subsequently hospitalized for depression, and the other succeeded in killing herself.

Many of my male peers in graduate school were married, but although I was also a wife, friendship with the other wives was problematic. Their lives revolved around supporting their husbands and taking care of a home and toddlers. Only one member of the department faculty was a woman—a superb teacher of history and systems who did not befriend the women students who might have benefited from her counsel. Another woman, Evelyn Hooker, did serve as a model for me, but our contact was infrequent; she was an adjunct professor who was never given full faculty status despite her reputation as an innovative scholar and fine teacher.

At psychology conferences I made further discoveries about the role of women in academia. We women students were ogled in elevators, invited to parties, and pursued by the most eminent of men within our discipline. I met men whose work I had been reading in my classes simply because I was a young woman and flattered by their attention. Only later did I understand how sexist and disrespectful these contacts were.

Despite the male environment, my experiences as a graduate student were positive and exciting. I became thoroughly hooked on learning theory, and cultural anthropology, my minor subject, taught me indelible lessons about human plasticity and variability. Exposure to empirical work generated by behaviorist hypotheses was consciousness raising, but I also remained respectful and appreciative of the work of Kurt Lewin. Years later, I wrote about the similarity between these two approaches (Lott & Lott, 1985). My major professor let me go my own wayward way and agreed to a dissertation that was a study of attitude formation and generalization, with attitudes defined as implicit goal responses and operationalized as color preferences. I demonstrated their acquisition by kindergarten children in a laboratory setting by using a mediated generalization learning paradigm. I have been told by those who appreciate this kind of research that this study (Eisman, 1955) is considered a classic.

I defended my dissertation in summer 1953 and followed my husband to his first academic job. Antinepotism sentiments were strong, so I began teaching extension courses—anything offered to me. Eager for full-time work, I turned to the public school system, just at the time that California was launching a program to keep "educable mentally retarded" children in the public schools. I talked my way into a job in special education at a junior high school and, despite my doctorate, had to take additional courses to earn a credential. I spent the next 2 years with 12 adolescents who had been diagnosed as mentally retarded in a converted storage room in the basement, entered only from the rear of the school. This was among the most enriching experiences of my life. I soon found that among my so-called "retarded" kids, some were simply hard of hearing, others were children of poor Mexican migrant workers with little English proficiency, and still others were just considered "bad" or unmanageable. I learned important lessons about intelligence and its testing, creativity, human potential, and social myths.

PERSONAL LIBERATION AND SOCIAL CHANGE

In summer 1956 I ended what had been, from the beginning, a painful marriage. My husband and I divided our meager assets equitably; we owned no property and had little savings. Fortunately, we also had no children. I had had an (illegal) abortion a year after our marriage on a table in the back room of a physician's office during early morning hours before his legitimate patients appeared. I am grateful to him, despite his uncaring manner and the dreadful pain, and to my ex-husband, who persuaded me to have the abortion. Terminating that pregnancy enabled me to get on with my life in a positive way.

At the American Psychological Association's convention in Chicago in 1956 I was hired as a temporary assistant professor at the University of Colorado. I filled my little blue Plymouth with clothes, books, and notes and drove off to Boulder from California, the first time in my life that I had ever driven such a distance by myself. I was launched on a grand adventure, about to become part of a university faculty, and to do something else I had never done before—live alone!

On my first day on the job, I met the man I married 2 years later. Four years older than I, he was just finishing his dissertation, because Army service during World War II had delayed his education while also making it possible through the GI Bill. The department said goodbye to me 2 years later, when they found the male "star" they had been searching for. I married and moved to Lexington, Kentucky. My husband had taken a job at the segregated state university, and I was hired to teach at the state college for Black students. During my 10 years at the college, I was the only White person on the faculty.

I had four children (one of whom died at birth) during these years, and adjustments in my teaching schedule made it possible for me to be my children's primary caregiver. The respectful and flexible treatment I received was not experienced by my husband; when he stayed home one afternoon each week to enable me to go to work some 30 miles away, he was derided by colleagues. In the early 1960s there were few options that would permit both my husband and me to work full time and raise a family. We settled on an arrangement in which he continued on the traditional tenure track in academia while also doing a good bit of the cooking, cleaning, and shopping. I did the heavy-duty child care and taught part time. We worked together on research grants and projects. We tried various child-care arrangements—home helpers, care in someone else's home, or day care. Other women psychologists during this period have had similar tales to tell (Chesler, Rothblum, & Cole, 1995).

In Kentucky, we were part of the civil rights movement. We held meetings, planned, marched, sang, and demonstrated. Sometimes we were threatened and some of us got arrested, but our small group of Congress of Racial Equality (CORE) activists succeeded in integrating the lunch counters, restaurants, movie theaters, and other public places in Lexington. Federal laws helped us eventually, but we had started the job in our city and done it well. So, along with my commitment to teaching and research and to my family, an important priority was social change. My experiences with CORE affected my work and thinking as a social psychologist and influenced my feminist activism in the succeeding years.

WORK AND FAMILY: PERSONAL, POLITICAL, AND PROFESSIONAL INTERSECTIONS

For a good number of years, when being a mother was my primary role, I was essentially outside the academic mainstream, doing what I called "professional hustling." I did not move into a full-time tenure track position in a department of psychology until 19 years after earning my doctorate. As an outsider, I pursued my research interests and retained my theoretical perspectives without thinking or worrying about potential threats to my career.

My three children are now scattered across the United States. My elder daughter, a technical writer, is the mother of a daughter. My second daughter is a family and immigration attorney, also the mother of a daughter. My son and youngest child, the father of three boys, is a coastal planner. I am proud of my children's values, the work that they have chosen to do, and the various paths they have taken. I have watched fearfully as my children made serious mistakes, but I have also seen them grow in competence, confidence, and concern for others and am heartened by the way they are living their adult lives.

I was not a traditional mother. Although the care, comfort, and happiness of my children were always my highest priorities, I continued my professional work, with varied schedules depending on the circumstances. When we moved to Rhode Island in 1969, I had a good record of published work.

Our move to Rhode Island brought us to the East Coast, where we had family attachments, and back to ocean and beaches. It was a good career move for my husband, and I was confident that I would find something worthwhile. However, the southern New England psychological community did not prove too hospitable (whether to women generally or to me personally, I could not be sure), and I discovered that my decision to be second author on joint papers with my husband because his name begins with an *A* and mine begins with *B* was cute personally to us but not very smart professionally for me.

During the lean years before I was appointed dean of a new college for 1st- and 2nd-year students in spring 1972, I did adjunct, underpaid teaching wherever I could. I developed a women's studies course (the first at the University of Rhode Island), taught the introductory psychology course to 900 students and then to 500 (at my request) students, and continued to do research. When asked to be the dean of the new college, an older and wiser me insisted on a tenure-track appointment in the Psychology Department as well. When my time for promotion to full professor arrived, my department chair asked me to wait—two of my male colleagues were up for promotion and he did not want them to have to compete with me. So I wrote a letter to my colleagues detailing my record (which compared more than favorably with many of theirs) and gained my department's support. This was another lesson in sexism and in what women must do in response to it.

Just as the time and place was right in Kentucky for civil rights activism, the time and place was right in Rhode Island for a feminist movement. I became part of a strong core of women faculty who developed a women's studies major, successfully sued the state and university administration for discrimination, and were instrumental in developing affirmative action and sexual harassment policies. We supported each other through tenure and promotion, strengthened each other as teachers and scholars,

and watched each other and our students grow personally and professionally and contribute to feminist theory and practice. A women's group
of friends that some of us started in 1970 still continues to meet.

The direction of my research and teaching has followed a fairly
consistent course. From the beginning, I have been interested in problems
of social justice as related to interpersonal behavior. I started off with
an interest in attitudes and then saw the relevance of interpersonal liking
for the study of group cohesiveness. What followed was systematic
empirical and theoretical work on the antecedents and consequences of
liking and disliking. I defined these concepts in behavioral terms embed-
ded in a learning theory framework and tested hypotheses in ecologically
meaningful contexts.

Later, I moved from a focus on gender attitudes and beliefs to
the study of what men actually did in the presence of women (i.e.,
discriminatory behavior). I proposed a social psychological model of
interpersonal sexism in which *prejudice* (attitudes), *stereotypes* (beliefs),
and *discrimination* (avoidance or distancing behavior) are conceptually
and operationally distinguished, and I tested hypotheses in studies of
sexist discrimination in face-to-face situations. Of the other major
threads in my work on gender, one is theoretical and integrative and has
involved feminist critiques of androgyny, exploration of the relationship
between the feminist perspective and social psychology, critical analyses
of "essentialist" and trait-bound theories of gender, and development
of a social learning model. Another thread has been research and writing
on sexual harassment, coercion, and assault.

Intertwined with my continuing development as a feminist social
psychologist is my identity as a social activist. In addition, the personal
story recounted here has been influenced by the many among my family,
friends, students, and colleagues with whom I have shared the quest to
understand the meanings of gender, ethnicity, and social class and their
consequences for experience and behavior.

I cannot remember a time when my attitudes and values were not
consonant with feminism. Those of us who were left-leaning political

activists before the mid-1960s generally referred to gender issues as "the woman question." But my feminist consciousness was inevitably influenced by the times and by my own particular life circumstances. I remember boasting, for example, as a very young married graduate student in the early 1950s that I would be happy to stay at home with small children and make my political contribution as a PTA mother and good community citizen. As I recall those words, I marvel at the strength of the social forces that led me to believe them. As it turned out, however, my personal and professional path was very different from what those words would lead one to expect.

My work on gender has paralleled my interest in the other social variables in our society associated with inequities in power—especially ethnicity and social class. Most recently, I have been teaching and writing primarily about poverty as it affects the lives of women and families in the United States. This focus on social class is intertwined with my work on women's issues. The distancing from poor people that is so evident in our national culture, politics, and institutions and that has such serious consequences for personal and national life (Lott, 2001, 2002a) has been at the forefront of my attention for the past decade as both citizen and psychologist.

I place myself proudly among those who identify as feminist scholars and practitioners within science, the humanities, and politics. My personal odyssey, in which personal, political, and professional work are intertwined, continues within the context of struggles for social justice, the challenge to psychology by feminist questions, and the development of a multicultural consciousness that appreciates diversity. Within the arena of multiculturalism, respect for people who are poor appears to be a difficult frontier, but some of us are determined that here, too, progress will be made.

4

Psychology, Social Class, and Resources for Human Welfare

With this chapter and the one that follows, we move to discussions of economic justice, which is where our personal, political, and professional journeys have led us. For feminist social psychologists, this focus seems inevitable. Because psychologists are committed to advancing human welfare, and because feminist psychologists are acutely aware of the antecedents and consequences of oppression, we must be concerned with issues of socioeconomic justice.

Our intention in this chapter is to outline the resources required for human welfare and to provide information on how low-income people in the United States are systematically impeded in their efforts to access them. These resources include food, housing, education, health care, fair and sustainable wages, and child care. This chapter draws on multiple and diverse sources of information about economic inequality and its correlates: data from psychological research, national statistics, reports by reputable journalists, and work from other social science disciplines.

SOCIAL CLASS INEQUITIES

Class inequity is not a new phenomenon in the United States. It is part of our historical development, beginning with the early White colonists, more than half of whom came to North America as servants (Zinn, 2003). However, the gap between rich and poor in this country is wider than it has been in more than 50 years (Moyers, 2004) and wider than in the older class-based societies of Europe and any other developed nation (Johnston, 2005a). In 1998, the income of the 13,000 richest American families was nearly equal to that of the 20 million poorest families (Atkinson, 2005). Statistics from the Center on Budget and Policy Priorities (I. Shapiro, 2005) indicate that from 1979 to 2002, while the after tax income of the top 1% of the population rose 111%, that of the middle fifth rose 15%, and that of the poorest fifth rose just 5%. In terms of taxes paid, the top 10th of 1% in this country had a reduced tax rate between 2002 and 2003 that was more than 10 times the rate reduction for middle-class taxpayers (cf. Johnston, 2005b). In 2004, big-company CEOs received an annual pay boost of 13% over the previous year, which earned them an average annual salary of $10 million (Morgenson, 2005).

Manhattan, in New York City, has the dubious distinction of having the greatest disparity between the rich and poor than any other county in the nation. In 2000, the top fifth of the population had an average annual income that was 52 times higher than the bottom fifth ($365,826 vs. $7,047; S. Roberts, 2005). Washington, DC, another of our country's great cities, has an infant mortality rate that is twice as high as that of Beijing; in 2002 this rate in our nation's capital was 11.5 per thousand live births as compared with 4.6 in China's capital (Kristof, 2005b).

It is thus not surprising that former President Carter said, when notified that he had won the 2002 Nobel Peace Prize, that his concept of human rights had grown to include "the right to . . . adequate health care, shelter, food, and to economic opportunity" (cf. Krasner, 2002, p. B6). However, dealing constructively with inequities continues to be hampered by myths. It is not the case, for example, that most of the poor in the United States live in urban ghettos. In fact only about 12% do. Half of all poor people in this country are White European American; fewer than one in five are in families headed by mothers who were never married; and in most poor families, there is at least one employed adult (Page & Simmons, 2000). Negative myths and untruths about the poor abound. Considerable data support the conclusion by Warren, Thompson, and Saegert (2001) that "poor and marginalized people have been literally vilified by the media and public officials" (p. 22).

What is true is that people in the United States today are more likely to finish their lives in the same social class into which they were born than was the case 30 years ago (Scott & Leonhardt, 2005). Class of origin is "the best predictor of adult educational and occupational achievement" (Jones, 2003, p. 804), despite our beliefs to the contrary and our adherence to the myth of class permeability. This myth, Jones (2003) argued, supports the perception that inequalities are due to personal deficiencies rather than to "institutional structures that tend to perpetuate privilege for higher status individuals" (p. 804). Miller (1996) noted that the belief in class permeability or upward mobility confuses aspirations with actual conditions of life.

In the presidential election rhetoric of 2004, both major parties consistently ignored the problems of the poor—wooing, instead, the so-called middle class. Policies and programs were presented as middle-class friendly, and the poor were forgotten or debased. Our political leaders may not see inequality as a high-priority problem, but we have the greatest level of inequality among Western countries. The United States "has more poverty and lower life expectancy than any other major advanced nation" (Krugman, 2002, p. 64). Swedes live, on average, 3 years longer than we do; Canadians, 2 years longer. The life expectancy for men in Costa Rica is greater than it is here. Krugman provided this comparison between Sweden and the United States: "Swedish families with children that are . . . poorer than 90 percent of the[ir] population— have incomes 60 percent higher than their U.S. counterparts" (p. 76).

As noted by Belle and Doucet (2003), the United States is unique in the industrialized world not only for our massive level of inequality, but also for the conviction that "both rich and poor deserve their fates" (p. 109).

Yet, low-income people share the same values and aspirations as those who are middle class. They want jobs, education, security, health care, recreation, and a good life (Lott & Bullock, 2001). An in-depth study (Holloway, Fuller, Rambaud, & Eggers-Pierola, 1997) of a sample of low-income mothers found that when they speak about their children, "their perceptions and concerns are ones shared by most parents, regardless of their social class" (p. 94). Steele (2002) reported that he found strong middle-class objectives among a sample of mothers interviewed in a homeless shelter and a valuing of independence and self-sufficiency even greater than in a sample of female students at Stanford. He concluded that the economic problems of the poor women were not due to personality deficits but to a lack of resources with which to cope with unreliable circumstances. Similarly, a study of poor teenagers in Philadelphia (see "Urban, Suburban Teens Have Same Worries," 2002) found them to have the same aspirations as their middle-class suburban counterparts: good schools, a chance to attend college, job training, jobs, and positive adult connections. A sample of low-income middle and high school students rated better books and computers and more after school activities as most likely to increase their chances for a positive future.

The resources required for a good, secure, and fulfilling life for women, men, and children are well known. Hobfoll (2002) has defined *resources* as what people value or as the "means to obtain centrally valued ends" (p. 307). He proposed that those "with resources are less likely to encounter stressful circumstances that negatively affect psychological and physical well-being" and "are more capable of solving the problems inherent in stressful circumstances" (pp. 317–318). In addition, those with resources are more likely to obtain more resources. The most basic requirements for a reasonably secure and satisfying life include adequate nutrition, housing, education, jobs that pay a living wage, access to health care, and child care.

Food

Poor families, like more affluent ones, require an adequate supply of nutritious food, but reports across the country continue to indicate an increased demand for emergency food and increased use of soup kitchens and food pantries. A report from the U.S. Conference of Mayors (cf. Becker, 2002) noted a 19.9% rise in food aid across the country, with working families being the neediest. Requests for emergency food have been steadily increasing since 1986, but in nearly two thirds of the 25 cities surveyed for the mayors' report, the amount of emergency food provided was being decreased and rationed. In 56% of the cities, emergency programs ran out of food and had to turn families away (cf. Relin, 2004). At the same time, one third of families eligible for food stamps do not get them (Shipler, 2004b).

Wollman (2002) examined data from 1995 through 1999 and found a 67% increase in the number of people who are hungry in this country, which is indicative of what he called *social negligence.* Who the hungry are and where they live are questions answered in data collected by America's Second Harvest (2002). These data show that among those who are hungry in the United States, 45% are classified as European American/White, 35% are African American, and 17% are classified as Latino; 53% are city dwellers, 32% are suburban dwellers, and 15% are rural.

The number of households experiencing *food insecurity,* a term used by the federal government to refer to limited or uncertain food availability, has been rising ("Food Security," 2004). According to data presented by the Department of Agriculture, in 2002 there were 12 million households in which some member of the family skipped a meal because of lack of food. Of the 34.9 million individuals in these families, more than

13 million were children (cf. Lu, 2004; Relin, 2004)—a devastating and shocking statistic.

Those lining up for emergency food baskets or coming to soup kitchens were described by a soup kitchen director in Connecticut (Lu, 2004) as primarily employed (80%) "mostly in low-wage jobs with no benefits . . . all sorts of invisible people that folks just refuse to see . . . gardeners, people living in the back of restaurants, [or] . . . the person working at the local grocery store" (¶12). A journalist who interviewed low-income families across the country described one mother who wouldn't take her children to shop for food because they grabbed for things she couldn't afford—like fruits and vegetables (Relin, 2004).

What the poor eat is typically lower in quality and less nutritious than what others eat. In one study (Topolski, Boyd-Bowman, & Ferguson, 2003), students judged the appearance and taste of fruit purchased from the same grocery chains in communities differing in socioeconomic status (SES). Produce from markets in the poorer neighborhoods was judged to be less fresh in both taste and appearance, suggesting to the investigators that their findings reflected "differential treatment" of consumers and "institutionalized discrimination" (p. 118). In addition, hungry families often buy foods high in calories but low in nutritive value (Associated Press, 2003) because such foods are cheaper and provide quick sources of energy ("High-Calorie Foods," 2004). One can get the same amount of energy from low-cost cookies as from far higher priced carrots or lettuce, which are luxuries for low-income families.

The relationship between lack of nutritionally adequate food and children's psychosocial functioning has been well established. Murphy, Wehler, et al. (1998) found, in a sample of inner-city public schools, that hungry children functioned more poorly than others on both behavioral and academic indices. Another study (Sampson, Dixit, Meyers, & Houser, 1995), of a large sample of low-income second- to fifth-grade students, reported that on any given day, 12% to 26% came to school without having eaten breakfast. Tests showed that a considerable propor-

tion of these children were deficient in nearly every important nutrient. There is a strong relationship between nutrition and brain development, both prenatally and postnatally (Thompson & Nelson, 2001).

Housing

The lack of adequate, affordable housing is another serious national problem—high on the list of concerns of the poor and the about-to-become poor. Heather Bullock's story in chapter 2 illustrates how housing issues can lead to family separation and to a further spiraling into poverty even for college-educated and formerly middle-class parents.

In a survey (Lott, 2002b) of 100 low-income women and men in one county in Rhode Island, the greatest number of respondents (92% of the women and 98% of the men) rated the issue of affordable housing as very important to them personally. The minimum wage, public transportation, and medical care came next in ratings of personal importance, but none of these came close to the importance of housing. Among households with the most serious housing needs, 57% are headed by women and 46% are headed by persons of color (Mulroy, 2002).

Poor, urban families are typically segregated into undesirable neighborhoods that are unseen by the affluent, who try to keep their distance from them. H. Epstein (2003) provided this description: "bricked-up abandoned buildings, vacant storefronts, broken sidewalks and empty lots with mangy grass overgrowing the ruins of old cars, machine parts and heaps of garbage" (p. 76). She cited a survey of four regions in the United States that found fewer parks in poor neighborhoods than in more affluent ones but three times as many bars. Evans (2004) described low-income neighborhoods as polluted, crowded, noisy, physically deteriorated, and dangerous, with inadequate public services of all kinds. Bernice Lott (who relates her personal story in chap. 3) remembers growing up in low-income urban neighborhoods in apartments with few windows, above retail stores, and facing busy outdoor vendors in crowded noisy streets. Cockroaches were ever present, to be seen scurrying away when one returned home and turned on the lights after an evening out.

Added to all this is the existence of environmental classism. In a study (Allen, 2001) of more than 2,000 counties in the United States, the level of toxic releases was found to be significantly related to the counties' social class status. Analysis of risk scores for industrial air pollution assigned to communities across the United States by a government research project found that neighborhoods where the residents were poorer and less educated had the highest pollution compared with neighborhoods where residents had a higher SES (cf. Pace, 2005).

Saegert and Evans (2003) wrote about the deleterious effects on health of housing with inadequate plumbing and no central heating; near waste sites; and with poor ventilation, pests, and lead paint. Yet housing, they pointed out, "is one of the largest expenditures in the budgets of low-income people . . . the poor pay so much . . . for housing that they must scrimp on other household needs" (p. 577). It is not surprising, given the conditions of housing in high-poverty communities, that a move to a better neighborhood will have positive effects. This was documented in a 3-year relocation study in five urban sites. The school achievement of teenage boys made significant gains after their families, having been chosen randomly for a chance to do so, moved to a low-poverty neighborhood (Leventhal & Brooks-Gunn, 2004).

A national study found that the average cost of rent and utilities for a two-bedroom apartment is $791 a month (cf. "Housing Too High for Many," 2003). To afford housing as well as food and other necessities, someone has to be earning $15.21 an hour (almost 3 times greater than the federal minimum wage). Even if a mother has been fortunate enough to find a place in a low-rent public housing project, she may be required to perform unpaid community service or face eviction. This was specified in the disingenuously named Quality Housing and Work Responsibility Act of 1998, signed into law by President Clinton (Chen, 2004), which called for community service every year by public housing residents who are not over 62 or disabled, not in school, or not working full time.

What counts as community service is to be determined by housing project administrators. This law has been unevenly implemented, but its existence illustrates how public housing renters are perceived as different from other recipients of federal assistance programs (e.g., tobacco farmers or corporations receiving subsidies).

Homelessness is another measure of social negligence. Wollman (2002) estimated that between 1995 and 1999, the homeless population in this country increased by 30%, and the U.S. Conference of Mayors (cf. Becker, 2002) reported that the need for emergency shelter in U.S. cities increased in 2002 by an average of 19% over the previous year. This is especially hazardous for women (Terrell, 2004); many homeless women are likely to be fleeing from domestic violence and then face the danger of assault on the streets.

The problem of homelessness can be illustrated by statistics from almost any major city or state. In Rhode Island, 2003–2004 marked an all-time high, for the 3rd year in a row, in the number of people entering emergency shelters. More first-time clients at the shelters were reported to be employed and to have more education and fewer substance abuse problems than previously, with a 9% increase in families (Ziner, 2005a). In New York City in the summer of 2002, the lack of housing was so severe that the city administration reopened an old jail to house homeless families, a move that evoked strong criticism and was blocked by a judge (Cooper, 2002). Another proposal was to house the city's homeless in retired cruise ships (B. Stewart, 2002). A quarter of New York City's homeless were given temporary shelter in furnished apartments in buildings with histories of dangerous code violations, including peeling paint and rat infestations (Kaufman, 2002). This scatter-site housing program is advantageous for landlords, who are paid $96 a day for every family and who net profits said to range from $600 to $1,000 per month on each apartment. In a temporary strategy, New York City has permitted homeless couples to sleep on benches or the floor of a former mental hospital ward without food or showers and with lights that remain on all night (Kaufman, 2005).

Education

The shortchanging of children from low-income families in the public schools is yet another structural and institutional tool that maintains privilege for some and oppression for others—that is, the status quo of social injustice. One study (cf. Schemo, 2002) found that school districts with the highest number of low-income students received an average of $1,000 less per student from state and local tax money than did school districts with the fewest poor students. A hard-to-believe example comes from Illinois, in which the highest-spending school district spent $19,361 more per student in 2005 than the lowest-spending district (Urrea, 2005). Most U.S. schools are funded through property taxes, which is by nature inequitable and enforces class differences between districts.

To statistics about financial support must be added the well-known discrimination experienced by low-income children and their parents in the public schools (for reviews of this literature, see Lott, 2001, 2003; Lott & Rogers, 2005). Respondents in a study by Adair (2002), like those in other studies, told "stories of the branding they received at the hands of teachers, administrators, and peers" (p. 457). Both of our personal stories (chaps. 2 and 3) describe the income-related embarrassment we felt during our own formative years. Many poor children have similar experiences in schools every day.

Teachers' expectations of students, which can become self-fulfilling prophecies, are different for children of poor and middle-income families. A survey of teachers in Rhode Island confirmed their low expectations for students of low-income parents (cf. Borg, 2004). The teachers, asked to assess academic potential from economic and ethnicity information, estimated that 72% of students from middle-class families had the ability to graduate from college but that only 48% of low-income students had the requisite academic potential.

Classist inequalities are seen in public schools across the country. School districts generally do little to keep low-income teenagers in school. Thus, the U.S. Department of Education found that "the drop-out rate

for the poorest 20 percent of students was six times that of the wealthiest 20 percent" (i.e., 10% vs. 2%; "More are Finishing High School," 2001, p. A2). Classist inequalities are also clearly seen in the physical condition of schools and in the quality of teachers. Phillips and Chin (2004) reported "disparities in teachers' education, credentials, experience, subject matter knowledge, and cognitive skills" that continue to disadvantage students in low-income schools (p. 510). The result, as Campbell (2002) has argued, is that unequal schools distribute knowledge unequally, which contributes to the maintenance of economic inequality and unequal opportunities. "One group of students learns skills and confidence and is prepared for their future, while other students learn their place (at the bottom)" (Campbell, 2002, p. 6). A recent study (cf. Scott & Leonhardt, 2005) found that the socioeconomic status of a child's family in the United States was a better predictor of school achievement than it was in France, Denmark, or the Netherlands.

The classism in public primary and secondary education is maintained in colleges and universities. One study (cf. "College Costs," 2002) found that low-income students needed loans in a third of states even to attend 2-year community colleges. Another study (cf. Lewin, 2002) assigned the nation's colleges the grade of D in affordability. Twelve states in this study, including New York, received an F; California was the only state to get an A. Among the most depressing findings was that only about half of community college students return for their second year. In addition, a congressional committee found that in 2002, among qualified low- and moderate-income high school graduates, nearly half did not enroll in any college (cf. Gaus, 2003). The chances of getting a college degree before age 24 varied from 1 in 2 for those from families earning more than $90,000 a year, to 1 in 10 for those from families earning $35,000 to $60,000, to 1 in 17 for someone from a family earning less than $35,000 (cf. Brooks, 2005).

The National Center for Public Policy and Higher Education reported that in 2000, poor families spent an incredible 25% of their income in order to have their children attend public 4-year colleges (cf. Steinberg, 2002). This is in sharp contrast to the 7% of annual income spent by middle-class families in educating their children. Pell grants covered only 57% of the tuition at public colleges in 1999, down from 98% in 1986. And a new federal formula for calculating financial aid has further reduced Pell Grant funds, which has resulted in 1.3 million college students receiving smaller grants and an estimated 89,000 not qualifying for any assistance; this is expected to have a domino effect on other types of aid, increasing the need for loans (Winter, 2004).

The situation at elite private colleges is bleak. "At 250 of the most selective colleges in the country, the proportion of students from upper-income families has grown" (Scott & Leonhardt, 2005, p. YT18). Students in the lowest economic quartile were found in one study (cf. Kahlenberg, 2004) to make up 3% of the students in the most selective 4-year colleges compared with 74% from the highest economic quartile. It is especially significant that the percentages of low-income and working-class students in these colleges were lower than if only grades and test scores had been used as admissions criteria. This reflects the continued use of legacy admissions, an affirmative-action program for the affluent. At Harvard University, 90% of the undergraduates are from families earning more than the national annual median income, and 77% come from households with incomes above $80,000 (Michaels, 2004).

Ironically, the wealthiest colleges receive significantly more federal dollars for financial aid than schools that have far greater numbers of poor students (Winter, 2003). Ivy League colleges get the most federal money for work-study jobs. In addition, at most colleges, the discounts that lower full tuition costs are more likely to go to wealthier than to poorer applicants (Zernike, 2003), because colleges use discounts to attract particular categories of students.

The barriers to higher education faced by the poor provide additional evidence of the institutional nexus of inequality pervasive in our nation. Affluent families not only have the necessary financial resources to send their children to college, but as Kirp (2004) pointed out, they know how to work the system. They send their children to college admission summer camps, enroll them in Scholastic Assessment Test preparation courses, and get advice from counselors. The result is that among qualified high school seniors, five out of six whose families earn more than $75,000 a year will enroll in a 4-year college, compared with fewer than 50% of those whose families earn less than $25,000. The consequence of colleges becoming more and more unaffordable for so many is that low-income students who never get to college end up with low-paying dead-end jobs and few possibilities for the future. Had Brooklyn College not been tuition free when Bernice Lott graduated from high school (see chap. 3), it is entirely possible that she might never have gone to college.

Low-income students who make it to college face considerable problems as they pursue academic achievement and prepare for a career. There is a wide gap in graduation rates between academically competent students from lower and higher income families. A College Board report (cf. Hong, 2005) indicated that among students with high test scores, those from families with the highest income finished college at more than twice the rate of those from the lowest-income families. One College Board analyst was quoted as saying that college completion has become more and more "not about academic preparation, [but] . . . about money" (Hong, 2005, p. A3). All college students currently face a situation of exploding textbook costs, with prices that have increased 186% in the past 20 years. This presents an especially difficult problem for low-income students. To read that "more and more students are resorting to an old alternative: the library" (Buss, 2005, p. BU8) reminds Bernice of the first 3 years of her undergraduate days when she never had the money to buy a single textbook and could read them only in the library.

An example of the differences in opportunities among students from different social classes is the growing importance of internships. For affluent students, unpaid internships pose no particular hardship and are widely used as ways to increase connections and gain experience on the path to careers, particularly in politics and the media. College students from working-class families cannot afford to spend a summer without earning money to help defray college costs and are thus at a serious disadvantage. In addition, internships often go first to those with network connections and family contacts and reflect cronyism, nepotism, and access associated with privilege (Coplin, 2005). As noted by journalist Cokie Roberts (quoted in J. Lee, 2004), the system makes "it ever more difficult for people who don't have economic advantages to catch up" (¶7). Both of us worked at various paying jobs throughout our college years during school semesters and summers. With barriers to college entry and lesser access to opportunities in college, upward mobility is a steep climb, often more dream than reality.

Work and Wages

Most poor people in our country are employed, but 31% of working women and 20% of working men earn less than $8 an hour. Twenty percent of all jobs in the United States pay less than a poverty-level wage for a family of four (see "Study Says 39 Million," 2004). Fourteen million people are working for $7 an hour or less (Herbert, 2002b).

Among the lowest-paid workers in New York State are home health aides, almost all of whom are women. They typically work for $6 or $7 an hour with no medical benefits, sick pay, or vacation days (Herbert, 2002a). Immigrant migrant workers are also among those most exploited. Although we tend to think of them as the farm workers who pick our fruits and vegetables, another group has emerged, primarily women who line up for day work in factories or homes. Bernstein (2005) has written about the women who "are not noticed by the weekday morning crowds" (¶1) in New York City as they wait to be "hired for a day's work at the minimum wage or less" (¶2) doing whatever is asked of them in factories, like cutting threads from jackets, or taking part "in the vast underground economy of domestic service" (¶5) in middle-class homes.

A campaign for living wage ordinances on city, county, or state levels has been pressing for requiring government employers and companies with government contracts or subsidies to pay their workers an hourly rate that will provide reasonable access to resources on a minimum-needs budget. (For example, $10.19 an hour has been proposed in Providence, RI; see Luna & Segal, 2003.) This movement is gaining strength. Baltimore passed the first such legislation in 1994; the states of Maine and Vermont link corporate subsidies to good wages; and in 2001 there were 60 cities with living wage ordinances and ongoing campaigns in 75 (Bruce, 2001).

Efforts in Congress to raise the federal minimum wage (from $5.15 per hour) have not been successful, even though this minimum has not been raised since 1997. Such a wage for 40 hours a week for 50 weeks yields an income of $10,500, which is almost half the poverty threshold for a family of four ($19,200 in 2004). A study in 2004 found that a full-time worker earning the federal minimum wage could afford rent and utilities for a one-bedroom apartment in only 4 of 3,066 counties in the U.S. To afford a two-bedroom apartment in 1,000 counties, a minimum wage earner must work more than 80 hours a week (see "Minimum Wage," 2004). As of this writing, neither Senator Edward M. Kennedy's proposed legislation to raise the minimum wage modestly in three steps to $6.65 ("ADA Spearheads," 2002) nor Representative George Miller's bill to raise it to $7.25 over 2 years (Stark, 2005) have been approved, which illustrates the strong tolerance for economic injustice among our policymakers and elected representatives in Washington. This is the case despite wide support for increasing the federal minimum wage revealed by opinion polls and higher minimums in 17 states and the District of Columbia (Broder, 2006).

It is significant that women in the United States are far more likely than men to be employed in jobs paying the lowest wages and are more likely to be poor in every adult category by age and education. In 2002, the poverty rate for single parents was 30.2%; within this group, single mothers were twice as likely to be poor as single fathers (NOW Legal Defense and Education Fund, 2003). In 2003, full-time female workers earned 75.5 cents for every dollar earned by a man, and the median annual earnings for women working full time was $30,724 compared with $40,668 for men (Institute for Women's Policy Research, personal communication, August 27, 2004).

Low wages are correlated with few benefits, poor conditions in the workplace, and few supports for working adults to fulfill their responsibilities to children and other family members. As Heymann (2000) documented, unlike workers in most other industrialized countries, who have access to paid family leave and publicly funded early childhood programs, workers in the United States do not. Thus "disparities in income are exacerbated by . . . dramatic disparities in working and social conditions" (p. 134).

In addition to the problems connected with wages and benefits, there is also a serious problem of unemployment. The official government unemployment rate has varied over the past few years (e.g., 6.4% in 2003 [Herbert, 2003b]; 5.6% in early 2004 [Krugman, 2004]), but these figures exclude large numbers of people who have given up looking for work, estimated to be more than 1.5 million at the end of 2003 ("Exhausting Federal Compassion," 2004). Other statistics indicate that 4.5 million people are working part time because they cannot find full-time employment (cf. Herbert, 2003c). Uncounted labor force dropouts move in with relatives, care for children, apply for disability benefits (Leonhardt, 2002), or make some other difficult life adaptation. Among the hardest hit are single, undereducated mothers for whom the unemployment rate is 18% ("The 12 Percent Problem," 2003) and young people between the ages of 16 and 24. Those who have spoken with these young unemployed have reported their frustration and anger but mostly just their sadness (Herbert, 2003a). Unemployment among Black men is at a crisis level—25%—a figure considered to be conservative (Herbert, 2004b). It is Black workers who have been hardest hit by the decline in unionized jobs. In the 1980s, 25% of all Black workers were union members; today only about one of seven has a union job. AFL-CIO President John Sweeney has called this "one of the little-known tragedies of the last five years" (Uchitelle, 2005, p. WK3)

Unemployment insurance has a time limit, and what one receives depends on the salary or wage at the last job held. State rules limit eligibility, and not all who are without a job qualify. It has been reported (cf. Jackman, 2003) that in 2001, 47% of jobless men across the country received unemployment insurance; the figure for jobless women was only 40%. These payments averaged about $230 a week (Armour, 2002).

Income Assistance

Public assistance is designed for those who cannot meet their basic needs through employment. Families who qualify earn less than what is designated as the poverty level. In 2004, this was $19,200 for a family of four. In that year, 37 million people, or 12.7% of the country's population, earned less than this threshold, and the median household income was $44,389 (Leonhardt, 2005). Of those living below the official poverty line, almost one third were children (Freyer, 2005). Living at and up to double the poverty line were an additional 54 million people ("Barely Staying Afloat," 2006). One in five workers in 2003 earned a median wage of less than $8.84 an hour, which would put a family of four in poverty. Among low-income families, it has been reported that 71% have at least one adult working and more than 50% are headed by a married couple (cf. Herbert, 2004c).

Among Black Americans, the poverty rate is twice as high as it is for the nation as a whole. The outrageous television pictures of the Hurricane Katrina victims in New Orleans in 2005 shocked the nation and the world, but as noted by journalist DeParle (2005a), the images simply "laid bare" what many already knew—our nation's "cleavage of race and class" (p. WK1). In New Orleans, of the 28% of the population living in poverty, 84% are Black (cf. DeParle, 2005a). And Native Americans remain the poorest ethnic group, despite the gambling businesses operated by some tribes, with an annual per capita income below $10,000 according to census data for 2000 ("Economic Data," 2005).

The official poverty level is still calculated the way it was when it was first introduced in 1963 (Bernstein, 2003): 3 times the cost of a low-income family's estimated food expenditures (on the assumption that the other two thirds of family income is spent on housing and clothing). Clearly this omits spending on child care, transportation, medicines, personal grooming products, and much more that middle-class people take for granted, like buying books or magazines, going to movies, renting videos, or taking vacations.

A study sponsored by several national foundations (cf. Herbert, 2004c) reported the following average annual expenses for a low-income family of four: renting a two-bedroom apartment in a major city, $8,000; food, $2,000; and transportation, $1,500. Subtracting these costs from a poverty-level income leaves little for clothing, child care, health, and other expenditures essential for a good life. It illustrates how easily, as Herbert (2004c) noted, poor families can be pushed over the edge by any misfortune.

Temporary Assistance for Needy Families (TANF) is a program established in 1996 as a way to end welfare programs, which had become increasingly identified by opponents with undeservingness and dependence. TANF continues to be reauthorized by Congress with the same antipoor features it had when it began, despite suggestions from many sources for ways of improving educational, vocational, and employment options for the poor (e.g., Blank & Haskins, 2001; National Women's Law Center, personal communication, March 26, 2004; Women's Committee of 100, personal communication, March 17, 2004). These suggestions have included eliminating the time limit for termination of benefits; expanding the definition of *work* to include postsecondary education, vocational education, and adult literacy programs; establishing federal benefit standards; enforcing equal pay laws; and increasing child-care funding. Former Congresswoman Patsy Mink (2002) said about TANF that it "set in motion a series of policy changes that degrade poor mothers, punish . . . and undermine their families . . . [and] it did nothing to move poor mothers out of poverty" (p. xxi).

Since passage of the TANF legislation, there has been a well-reported reduction in state welfare caseloads, but there has been no significant shift in the numbers of families living below the poverty line. Access to affordable housing has gotten worse, and emergency food needs have sharply increased. In Washington State, for example, according to Children's Defense Fund data for 1998 (cf. Pearce, 2002b), although there was a significant reduction in the welfare roll, among full-time workers, 30% had their phones cut off, 18% had utilities shut off, and 22% became homeless.

On any given day, 40% of former welfare recipients (who are primarily mothers) have no job (Edelman, 2002). A federal assistant secretary for families and children has been quoted as agreeing that 10% to 15% of those who have left the welfare system since 1996 are significantly worse off than they had been before (cf. Kaufman, 2003). Those who are working earn, on average, a bit less than $8 an hour for a 35-hour workweek and thus make around $14,000 a year. What has been learned from the 1996 law is that having a job is not the same as earning a living wage.

New Zealand repealed its similar workfare program because it failed to give people "real jobs at real wages" ("New Zealand," 2002). Studies found that employers took advantage of those in the program, relying on them as a source of low-wage labor and making it difficult for them to move into good jobs. This is most certainly also the case in the United States, where similar abuses have been documented.

Welfare assistance in the United States (both pre- and post-TANF) has occurred within a system that tends to undermine the self-respect of its recipients. Although most of us can insist on a search warrant before permitting an officer into our homes, welfare mothers must allow entry to social workers, thus "fork[ing] over citizenship rights for the price of a welfare check" (Smith-Madsen, quoted in Adair, 2002, p. 460).

Health Care

The resource to which low-income people in this country have the least access is health care. As the only industrialized country without a national health system, we spend $5,800 a year per person on health care (Hellander, 2003), more than 2 times the average expenditure in other industrialized countries. Despite its high cost, our system does not provide the highest quality of care. The United States ranked 12th in a comparison among 13 countries in 2000 on 16 health indicators (cf. Herbert, 2004a). Canada has surgical survival rates that are higher than those in the United States (Sullivan, 2002–2003), and other developed countries have infant mortality rates that are half of the rate in the United States (6.8 deaths per 1,000 live births). Our high rate of infant mortality is attributed to the inadequate access to health care in poor communities ("Infant Mortality," 2003). Among the countries with better infant survival rates than ours (we are 41st in the world) are Singapore, Cuba, China, Sweden, and Japan (Kristof, 2005a). In the western hemisphere we have the third-worst rate of vaccination in children, and in the world we rank 16th in female life expectancy and 17th in male life expectancy (Frisof, 2004).

New voices are being raised in support of the only sensible and serious way to assure health care for all, a single-payer system similar to that in Canada and Europe (e.g., Cook, 2005; Liebman, 2005). Among these voices is the Physicians' Working Group for Single-Payer National Health Insurance (2003). This group has called for abolishing financial barriers to health care through a plan that "would cover every American for all medically necessary services, including long-term care, mental health and dental services, and prescription drugs and supplies" (p. 799). With such an equitable plan, "clinical decisions would be driven by science and compassion" (p. 802), and lives would be saved. The authors of the plan noted that it was endorsed by close to 8,000 physicians and medical students. Other new proponents of a single-payer system that would eliminate the role played by insurance companies have been more surprising. An editorial in the conservative *Providence Journal* ("It's No Insurance Panacea," 2004), for example, recently posed the question: "When are we going to cut red tape and costs, and improve health-care equity by extending Medicare to everyone?" (p. B4), and the state of

Rhode Island has created a commission to study a single-payer system (Gemma, 2004). Representative John Conyers of Michigan has introduced a bill into Congress, drafted by a group of physicians, that would expand Medicare to all residents of the United States, cover medications, and provide parity for mental health services (Hellander, 2003). Unfortunately, labor unions have not yet joined the call for a national health program because, as Gold (2003) argued, health benefits are a "bargaining chip, and . . . selling point" in organizing (p. 9), and as Fitch (2005) pointed out, many unions have established their own health insurance companies.

Nearly 60 million people in this country are without health insurance at some point during any given year (Pear, 2003), more than half of whom are in the workforce. The numbers of those who are uninsured has continued to rise steadily and reached 46 million people at the beginning of 2005 (about 16% of the country's population; Broder, 2005). In 2004, this group included 20.6 million full-time workers, 11.4% of all children (Freudenheim, 2004), as well as more than 17 million women (Institute for Women's Policy Research, personal communication, August 27, 2004). Within the group of the uninsured are 33% of all Latinos and 19% of African and Asian Americans (Physicians' Working Group, 2003).

A study by the Kaiser Family Foundation (cf. Krugman, 2005a) found that uninsured people are 3 times more likely to postpone medical care and leave prescriptions unfilled than those who are insured. Patients without insurance are often charged more by doctors than those with insurance. If there is no medical emergency, an uninsured person may well be charged more for hospital care, even in nonprofit hospitals, than what an insurance company pays for their insured clients (Abelson & Glater, 2004; Kolata, 2001). It is not just the uninsured who face high medical costs. One study found that among insured low-income families, because of copayments and other out-of-pocket costs, 10% of chronically ill patients did not get care, 30% delayed getting care, and 43% did not fill prescriptions (cf. "Double Pinch," 2004).

Basic facts about the health insurance business are not well known. For example, although the U.S. Medicare program and the Canadian national health service spend less than 3.2% annually on overhead costs, private health insurers and HMOs spend 12% of the premiums for overhead (Physicians' Working Group, 2003). Money is spent on utilization review companies, lawyers, consultants, billing agents, and so on, so that half the money taken in never gets to the health providers—the doctors and hospitals (Angell, 2002). According to a study by a physicians' group (Woolhandler, Campbell, & Himmelstein, 2003), administration costs are 31% of health care expenses in the United States compared with 16.7% in Canada.

Angell (2002) argued that "we treat health care as a commodity . . . [and] the criterion for receiving it is ability to pay, not medical need" (p. WK13). Although health care is considered a public good and a human right in many parts of the world and was so recognized by the United Nations more than 50 years ago in its Universal Declaration of Human Rights, the United States regards it as a personal and purchasable market commodity (Frisof, 2004). The continuing serious consequence is that in the United States, SES is a strong and reliable predictor of health outcomes (Gallo & Matthews, 2003) and all causes of death regardless of ethnicity, gender, and age (Whitfield, Weidner, Clark, & Anderson, 2002). As noted by Belle and Doucet (2003), "each increment in income is associated with improved odds of experiencing a healthy and long life" (p. 104). House (2002) explained the situation simply: "Exposure to and experience of major health risk factors are structured by socioeconomic position" (p. 135).

Analyses of data in Massachusetts (Hudson, 2005) for 1994 to 2000 supported the conclusion of a "strong and consistent negative correlation between socioeconomic conditions and mental illness . . . regardless of the particular indicator of SES or type of mental illness examined" (p. 16). Research also has pointed to the role played by negative emotions, because not surprisingly, SES has been found to be inversely related to

symptoms of anxiety, depression, feelings of hopelessness, and greater exposure to stress (Gallo & Matthews, 2003).

Correlations between income, education, and occupation and mental and physical health outcomes continue to be reported. Matthews (2005) has noted that chronic heart disease in adulthood can be predicted from early childhood SES, and SES has been implicated in a host of chronic diseases (H. Epstein, 2003). Data summaries have supported the conclusion that "class is a potent force in health and longevity in the United States," with higher income people less likely "to have and die of heart disease, strokes, diabetes and many types of cancer" (Scott, 2005, ¶6). One study found that underemployed or unemployed people were 4.5 times more likely than others to get sick after being exposed to a cold virus (cf. Clay, 2001). Another example is from a study of breast cancer, which found income related to both the quality of medical care and the likelihood of a fatal outcome (cf. "Death Rate," 2002). An analysis of national data to examine disparities between the health care of Blacks and Whites found that socioeconomic conditions were a greater cause of these disparities than race (cf. Payne, 2004). Data of a different kind came from a natural experiment (Costello, Compton, Keeler, & Angold, 2003) that took place in a rural area in North Carolina. Researchers found, among a sample of 1,420 children from the ages of 9 to 13 followed over 8 years, that those whose families moved out of poverty after the building of an Indian casino showed a 40% decrease in conduct and defiant disorders (e.g., bullying, temper tantrums, stealing, and vandalism).

Although such findings should come as no surprise to psychologists, little systematic attention is typically paid to the day-to-day erosion of health among the poor and the day-to-day frustrations experienced in attempting to access the health care provided in clinics serving the poor. Perez-Pena (2005) spent 16 months inside such a clinic in the Bronx, New York, and documented how good intentions were often undermined by "inscrutable rules, daunting paperwork, [and] human frailties"

(p. A1). In Bernice's story in chapter 3, there are memories of crowded waiting rooms and overworked, unsmiling medical personnel that she experienced as a child as she and her mother waited for attention in clinics in Brooklyn. Adair (2002) wrote poignantly from her own experience about how often children in poor families are hurt and ill and how, without medical care, "small illnesses and accidents spiraled into more dangerous illnesses and complications" (p. 456). Like others, she wrote about the constant exhaustion experienced by low-income adults trying to deal with an overwhelming array of barriers. The conditions in which poor families must live are destructive to the spirit, to psyches, and to bodies.

Child Care

An issue of primary importance to women, which should also be but often is not a central focus for men, is child care. Tax credits provide minimal assistance, but not to families who do not owe income taxes. An analysis of relevant data showed that more than 25% of children (and 50% of all Black children) are in families that do not fully qualify for the federal child tax credit because the family income is too low; half get partial credit, and half get nothing (cf. DeParle, 2005b). The federal Child Care and Development Block Grant is helping just one in seven children who are eligible (National Women's Law Center, personal communication, January 27, 2004), and in 2005 there were 37 states that had set child-care reimbursement rates below the level that federal guidelines recommended (National Women's Law Center, personal communication, September 20, 2005). This woeful state of affairs has been well known, as illustrated by a letter to the Senate leadership in which 40 senators wrote that "the child care crisis in our states is deepening, as waiting lists grow longer, eligibility levels are reduced, and fewer parents are able to find or afford the child care that allows them to get—and keep—a job" (C. H. Smith, personal communication, October 15, 2002).

Bergmann (2002) proposed that child care for families at or below the poverty line be completely subsidized by public funds, with other families above the poverty line paying no more than 20% of their income. Another plan that she outlined, proposed by a group of large corporations, the Committee for Economic Development, calls for the federal and state governments to share the cost of providing all children with free classes starting at age 3 and to offer afternoon and summer hours for children of employed parents. This plan is modeled after a program in France.

The National Women's Law Center (personal communication, May 4, 2004) has reported strong support for publicly funded prekindergarten programs. They cited a poll conducted in 2004, which found that most women of all political identifications favor preschool programs (84% of Democrats, 69% of Republicans, and 71% of Independents); another poll found similar positive attitudes expressed by 66% of a sample of registered voters of both genders. They also noted that 10 states (California, Florida, Georgia, Illinois, Massachusetts, Michigan, New Jersey, New York, Ohio, and Texas), recognizing the benefits of providing early childhood education, offer public prekindergarten for all children.

INEQUALITIES AND POWER

Power, in the words of Prilleltensky (2003), is identified with "the capacity and opportunity to fulfill or obstruct personal, relational, or collective needs" (p. 21). Those with less access to resources who find formidable barriers in their paths as they move toward obtaining what is needed for the welfare of themselves and their families have less power than those with greater access. Lemieux and Pratto (2003) argued that "poverty is a product of human social relationships ... [of] how much or how little people value others in relation to themselves" (p. 147). These relationships help determine the distribution of resources, the differential access to which defines differences in power. It is this "deprivation of power" that the Nobel Prize–winning economist Amartya Sen proposed as the definition of poverty (cited in Moreira, 2003, p. 71).

The relative lack of power is central in understanding the role that poverty plays in everyday lives and how poverty is linked to the experience of trauma and to sociopolitical violence (Moreira, 2003). Power is derived from access to resources, to all that is required for a good and secure life. Differences in power have immediate and long-lasting consequences for individuals and communities. It has been proposed (Keltner, Gruenfeld, & Anderson, 2003) that high power encourages approach behaviors, attention to rewards, and positive emotions, whereas low power does the opposite. Low power results in inhibited and constrained behavior, with attention focused on threats. It is predictable, then, as data indicate, that income predicts levels of voting and political participation and that the more affluent have more influence on societal decisions and policies (e.g., R. B. Freeman, 2004; Miller, 1996; Verba et al., 2004).

Blackman (1996) argued that power is used to constrain those who do not fit the middle-class norm and for the purpose of social exclusion. Thus, terms like *underclass* are invented to describe the poor—who, as Gans (1996) suggested, some "would like to see disappear with verbal magic" (p. 90). The system that turns people into a labor surplus, Gans noted, then labels them as "lazy and otherwise morally deficient and undeserving" (p. 99). Such beliefs about the poor are well documented (e.g., Bullock, Wyche, & Williams, 2001; Cozzarelli et al., 2001). In much of the psychological literature, argued Walkerdine (1996), social class is implicit in approaches to and as ways of regulating "normality and pathology" (p. 357; see also Landrine, 1991). Those who are excluded from one's range of justice or consideration of fairness (typically persons considered different from oneself), those who are stigmatized and negatively stereotyped and belittled, and those with little power are vulnerable to being treated badly and with disregard and unconcern about the harm being done to them (Hafer & Olson, 2003; Opotow, 1990).

There has been a clear decline in social mobility in the United States. Zinn (2003) reported findings from a Carnegie Endowment study that two young people with equal intelligence test scores but from different social class backgrounds will have very different futures: "The child of a lawyer . . . was four times as likely to go to college, 12 times as likely to finish college, and 27 times as likely to end up in the top 10 percent of American incomes" (p. 663).

Although mobility has lessened, there has been a rise in low-wage jobs that lead nowhere. The people in dead-end jobs are usually invisible, like laundry workers in New York City who wash, dry, and fold in back rooms for far less than the minimum wage and who may work a 72-hour week (Greenhouse, 2004). Shipler (2004a) described such workers as "part of the hidden America"—those who "sew clothes, clean offices and harvest fruit . . . [who] serve Big Macs and stack merchandise . . . package lights . . . [or] assemble books of wallpaper samples" (p. 22). The majority of these low-income workers are women and mothers.

Beyond gender, there is a reliable relationship between social class and ethnicity in this country. This is revealed by an analysis of the wealth of households (assets that include a home, a car, and savings minus debts). In 2002, a study found that the median net worth of White households ($88,000) was 14 times that of Black households and 11 times that of Hispanic households (cf. "Study Says White Families' Wealth Advantage Has Grown," 2004). This study also found that nearly 33% of Black families, 26% of Hispanic families, and 11% of White families were in debt or had zero assets. These figures indicate the precarious economic position of large numbers of people within the United States.

Halstead (2003) has listed the "bests" and "worsts" in this country compared with other nations. In the worsts column are poverty, economic inequality, life expectancy, infant mortality, and health care coverage. Not surprisingly, this matches the experiences of low-income people. The American Psychological Association's (APA's) Urban Initiatives Office (1999) collected personal stories from a sample of poor single mothers "fighting for survival and for a way out of poverty" (p. 1). Each was asked what she thought needed to be done. Their recommendations included a guaranteed minimum income; ensuring that TANF benefits cover rent, electricity, and other basics; affordable housing and transportation; enough to eat; quality child care; education; health insurance; and removing the stigma from poverty.

THE SIGNIFICANCE OF SOCIAL CLASS FOR PSYCHOLOGY

How can such concerns of low-income women and men receive serious attention within psychology? Despite the repeated documentation that poverty provides cumulative and multiple stresses and risks and "is harmful to the physical, socioemotional, and cognitive well-being of children, youths, and their families" (Evans, 2004, p. 88), psychologists have not made the study of social class a high priority. Although APA's Public Interest Directorate "continues to support and promote efforts to apply the science and profession of psychology to advance human welfare" (APA, 2003, p. 518), it included nothing about the poor in a list of initiatives, and it asked the Council of Representatives to eliminate the office of Urban Initiatives (which was done). Similarly, the focus of the National Multicultural Conference and Summit (see APA, 2005) was on race, ethnicity, sexual orientation, and disability, but, as was the case in previous summits, there was no mention of social class in the flyer announcing the conference. In discussing the lack of serious and consistent attention to diversity in psychology, Tomes (2005) noted that psychology textbooks "have little to say about aging, disability, gender, sexual orientation or race/ethnicity" (p. 37), leaving out, once again, any mention of social class. There are positive signs of change, however. In February 2005, APA's Council of Representatives authorized a 2-year task force on SES and its relation to health and human welfare; this task force has been gathering information and preparing recommendations.

How can psychologists and feminists fail to be interested in the lives of poor women and their families, who provide us with incredible examples of resilience? As voiced by Adair (2002), poor people manage to survive while they "live on the unlivable and teach . . . [their] children love, strength, and grace" (p. 467). There is much to be learned from how poor people manifest agency in the face of "forbidding forces" (Prilleltensky, 2003, p. 41) and how they continue to work within individual families or community groups to disrupt systematic efforts by the more powerful to maintain the status quo of inequity in access to resources.

Psychologists need to study and write about the strengths, the creativity, and the knowledge and skills of poor people and about their hopes, dreams, and attitudes, and we need to document how they negotiate meaningful lives. The objective is not to romanticize the poor but to bring the complexity of such lives into respectful and clear focus. We must ask what the probable consequences are of the pessimism, alienation, and sense of betrayal and disrespect that are experienced by many. We must go to the experts, the poor, just as feminist psychologists have gone to women, to find out what is required for a good life. It is not surprising that low-income people, who are experts on their own lives, identify good jobs, health care, quality education, and neighborhoods with parks that are safe and clean as aspects of a good life.

Much evidence supports the assertions of those like Zafirovski (2003) that "big money is the prime force of politics" (p. 75) in the United States and determines who has influence. Krugman (2002), too, argued that "money buys political influence; used cleverly, it also buys intellectual influence" (p. 141) and that "big rewards are reserved for people with the right connections" (p. 142). If that is indeed the case, how can the connections be increased between low-income people and those in positions of power? How can the concerns of low-income people receive serious attention from policymakers who are affluent and who have been elected or appointed on the basis of financial and political support from others like themselves? What tools can psychologists use to advance an activist agenda for economic justice? How can we increase the sense of outrage among the economically comfortable about what Putnam (2001) has called "the most urgent moral problem in contemporary

America" (p. xv)—that is, the persistence of poverty and inequality? These questions need to be addressed if we wish to be effective in promoting human welfare for all.

Among all within the community of psychologists, we feminists who have researched, written, and theorized about gender oppression can and must extend our work to include the oppression of other groups. We have begun to do so in our serious inclusion of ethnicity, disability, and sexual orientation as categories vital to the understanding of life experience and behavior. We can enrich our work and potential effectiveness even further by raising social class to the theoretical and empirical position it merits. In the next chapter, we examine the attitudes and beliefs that constitute the ideological roots of economic injustice and that influence public policy.

5

The Psychology and Politics
of Class Warfare

The previous chapter documents the challenges that poor women
and their families face in the United States: limited access to quality
health and child care; substandard housing and homelessness; under-
funded schools and fewer educational possibilities; dangerous, low-wage
work; inadequate unemployment and welfare programs; and ultimately,
compromised life chances. Public outcry against such injustices seldom
parallels the magnitude of the problems they create. Policies that widen
the economic gap, whether tax initiatives that benefit the wealthy at the
expense of the poor or policies that restrict access to welfare benefits
for low-income families, enjoy relatively strong support from most
Americans.

This chapter examines the ideological roots of economic injustice
by looking at the attitudes and beliefs that underlie the social and political
exclusion of poor and working-class women and their families from the
resources needed to promote well-being. Attention is paid to how the
term *class warfare* is used in political discourse and how it is related to
institutional power; the biases that pervade public attitudes; and ultimately, social policy. Social psychological research on stereotyping,

intergroup relations, and media framing is used to inform our analysis, as are feminist and sociological analyses of the maintenance of power. It is our hope that exposing the tools of "class warfare" will be a catalyst for dismantling their effectiveness.

CLASS WARFARE AND THE POLITICS OF DIVIDEND TAXATION

With top corporate executives earning more than 1,000 times the pay of average workers (Krugman, 2002), it is perhaps not surprising that accusations of class warfare punctuate political rhetoric in the United States. Charges of class warfare are used frequently to silence opposition to policies that disproportionately benefit the wealthy rather than to challenge rising inequality (for analyses of inequality, see Keister & Moller, 2000; T. M. Shapiro & Wolff, 2001). As Krugman (2005b) observed, "to suggest that sustaining programs like Social Security, which protects working Americans from economic risk, should have priority over tax cuts for the rich is to practice 'class warfare'" (p. A21).

Class warfare rhetoric dominated the highly partisan debates that occurred in early 2003 following the Bush administration's proposed elimination of the tax on dividends (the income that corporations pay to their stockholders). Estate and capital gains taxes and the taxation of personal income from dividends are among the most progressive aspects of the U.S. tax system, but campaigns against taxing these forms of income at higher rates than other types of income (e.g., wages) jeopardize their redistributive potential (Friedman, 2005).

The Bush administration's plan to eliminate the dividend tax was not adopted, but the tax rate on dividend income was reduced from 38.6% to 15.0% through 2008 (Citizens for Tax Justice, 2004). At a cost of $148 billion, the consequences of dividend and capital gains tax cuts are far reaching (Friedman, 2005). With decreased government revenue to support social programs and other federal spending, the wealthiest

1% of the U.S. population benefits the most from these tax cuts (Johnston, 2005a). The Center on Budget and Policy Priorities (CBPP; A. Lee & Friedman, 2003) estimated that in 2003, households making over $1 million a year would be eligible for an average tax cut of $93,500, whereas middle-income households would receive an average tax cut of only $217. Approximately 36% of households were projected to receive no tax cut, and 53% were estimated to receive $100 or less. Collectively, the Bush administration's tax cuts have eroded the progressive nature of taxes to such an extent that "the 400 taxpayers with the highest incomes—a minimum of $87 million in 2000 ... now pay income, Medicare and Social Security taxes amounting to virtually the same percentage of their incomes as people earning $50,000 to $75,000" (Johnston, 2005a, ¶13). It is also striking that "those earning more than $10 million a year now pay a lesser share of their income in these taxes than those making $100,000 to $200,000" (Johnston, 2005a, ¶14).

The skewed impact of reducing dividend taxes is inevitable given that only 49.5% of U.S. households own stock (primarily through employer-sponsored retirement plans and mutual funds), and half of these have equity holdings worth $50,000 or less (Huntley, 2002). Yet, the elimination of the dividend tax was promoted by the Bush administration with claims that it benefited middle-income families. Analyses suggesting otherwise were branded as class warfare. In a speech President Bush gave while visiting a small flag company in Virginia, he argued that his policies are fair to all income groups:

> You hear a lot of talk in Washington, of course, that this benefits so-and-so or this benefits this, the kind of class warfare of politics. Let me just give you the facts, that under this plan a family of four with an income of $40,000 will receive a 96% reduction in federal income taxes. (quoted in Stevenson & Stolberg, 2003, ¶3)

But the $1,333 tax reduction that President Bush claimed a hypothetical family of four would have gained under the administration's plan pales in comparison with the potential windfall for the wealthy if the dividend tax were fully eliminated. For example, the three largest share-holders among officers and directors at Fortune 100 companies would have each enjoyed an average tax cut of $400,000 from the elimination of the dividend tax (U.S. House of Representatives Committee on Government Reform, 2003).

Democratic Party leadership sought to raise awareness of the disparate impact of the elimination of the dividend tax and argued that large corporations and the wealthy would benefit most (U.S. House of Representatives Committee on Government Reform, 2003). The Bush administration responded by accusing Democrats of engaging in class warfare. In turn, Democrats attempted to show the hypocrisy of such a claim. Representative Charles B. Rangel of New York, the senior Democrat on the House Ways and Means Committee, said in an interview, "It is class warfare, and they've declared it. . . . Here the president kicks the hell out of the poor and tells us we're guilty of class warfare" (quoted in Stevenson & Stolberg, 2003, ¶17). In a memo circulated to House Democrats, Rangel observed that *class warfare* is a phrase that "seems vaguely un-American" and, according to reporters, "compared its use in the tax debate to the way people in the civil rights movement had once been called communist sympathizers." Rangel called on Democrats "not to be intimidated" (Stevenson & Stolberg, 2003, ¶18).

Rangel was concerned that being accused of class warfare would lead his fellow Democrats to support the elimination of the dividend tax. This concern highlights a fundamental paradox: Those who question the legitimacy of policies that disproportionately benefit the wealthy are labeled as engaging in class warfare, whereas those who support the policies most strongly are not so labeled. Many of our punitive institutions, for example, the penal (Haney & Zimbardo, 1998) or welfare (Delgado, 2002; Piven & Cloward, 1993) systems, institutions that disproportionately affect the lives and life chances of low-income people, are not overwhelmingly recognized as instruments of class warfare, despite the harm they cause. Using the politics of class warfare rhetoric, powerful groups attempt to justify oppressive policies and then label their critics as class warriors. If psychologists are to effectively advocate for social change, it is essential that we understand the social psychological processes involved in transforming honest talk about disparity into a political liability that undermines the credibility of equity advocates.

LANGUAGE IN THE SERVICE
OF SOCIAL HIERARCHIES

Reduced dividend taxation (in conjunction with other tax breaks for top earners) is only one example of how current economic policies are widening the class divide. Current environmental policies make it easier for corporations to pollute and destroy air and water quality in low-income communities (National Resources Defense Council, 2003), affordable housing programs remain under assault (L. Freeman, 2002; Roach 2002), and welfare "reform" policies punish the poor (Delgado, 2002; Mink, 2001). Attempts by conservatives to dismantle the safety net are not political anomalies. Rather, they are grounded in a long legacy of institutional classism in the United States, including our adoption of the English Poor Laws and the 1970s mobilization of corporations to weaken unions and workplace protections (Katz, 2001; "Labor Pains," 2005; Piven & Cloward, 1993). A vast interlocking system of punitive laws, policies, and social structures is the true weapon of class warfare. Yet, policies that benefit the rich but hurt the poor are rarely framed as such in mainstream media outlets. As Marx and Engels (1932/ 1938) noted,

> The ideas of the ruling class are in every epoch the ruling ideas: i.e., the class, which is the ruling material force of society, is at the same time its ruling intellectual force ... [and] is compelled, ... merely in order to carry through its aim, to represent its interest as the common interest of all the members of society ... it will give its ideas the form of universality, and represent them as the only rational, universally valid ones. (pp. 39–41)

The proposed elimination of the dividend tax is packaged as an economic stimulus for families of all incomes, despite extensive evidence to the contrary. The construction of elite interests as universally shared ones is also fostered by extensive news coverage of stock market and business news as central concerns.

Over the past 20 years, the ability of elites to control public discourse and shape public opinion has been enhanced by the concentration of media ownership by major corporations (Bagdikian, 2004; Compaine & Gomery, 2000; Croteau & Hoynes, 2001; Hatch, 2003). In 1983, 50 corporations controlled the majority of the media; today there are just five giant media conglomerates (Bagdikian, 2004). Corporations dominate even the newspaper industry, historically among the least concentrated forms of media (Bagdikian, 1997). At the end of World War II, 80% of daily U.S. newspapers were independently owned, but by 1989, corporations controlled 80% of newspapers. Commenting on the threat that highly concentrated ownership poses to an open, accessible media operating in the public interest, Bagdikian (1997) argued that

> the reporting of news has always been a commercial enterprise and this has always created conflicts of interest. But the behavior of the new corporate controllers of public information has produced a higher level of manipulation of news to pursue the owners' other financial and political goals. In the process, there has been a parallel shrinkage of any sense of obligation to serve the noncommercial information needs of public citizenship. (pp. xi–xii)

Feminist scholars (Bohan, 1993; Stapleton, 2001) have written extensively about the power of language to create and maintain, not simply reflect, social hierarchies. Discourse analysis has proved to be a powerful tool for revealing the biases that pervade the dominant framing of contested social issues. Feminist analyses of mainstream representations of motherhood and abortion (Feagan, 1996; Gregg, 1994; Hopkins, Reicher, & Saleem, 1996; Potgieter, 2003) have yielded insight into gender, power, and the values and behaviors that come to be labeled "normative" versus those labeled "problematic." Similar insights regarding class and power can be gained by examining the partisan exchanges surrounding proposals to eliminate the dividend tax.

THE UNIVERSAL MIDDLE CLASS AND THE MYTH OF MERITOCRACY

Conservatives seem to understand and use to their advantage the hesitancy of many people in the United States to talk openly about class or to critique economic privilege. This reluctance is evident in former President George H. W. Bush's comment that class is "for European democracies or something else—it isn't for the United States of America. We are not going to be divided by class" (quoted in Mantsios, 1992, p. 96). Such remarks illustrate two seemingly inconsistent but complementary beliefs about social class that dominate our political landscape: (a) The United States is a classless society, and (b) almost everyone in the United States is middle class (Mantsios, 2004; Miller, 1995). Both beliefs obscure the power of those at the top of the financial hierarchy and the struggle of those who are economically insecure.

The social construction of a so-called universal middle class reflects what Miller (1995) referred to as a confusion of "aspiration with condition" (p. 100). Psychologists have conceptualized this phenomenon as a discrepancy between objective indicators of class status (e.g., income, education, occupation, neighborhood) and a subjective sense of class belonging. In the United States, this disconnect is evident in a tendency toward "upward" self-identification, most notably to identify as "middle class" even when educational or occupational background is inconsistent with objective indicators of middle-class status (Kelley & Evans, 1995). A study (Goodman et al., 2000) comparing patterns of class identification among working- and upper middle class adolescents found that 83% of working-class youth self-identified as middle or upper middle class despite their working-class family backgrounds. Upper middle class respondents were significantly more likely than their working-class peers to identify correctly with their objective class positions, with 74% identifying with middle-class groups. No one in the middle-class group misclassified themselves as working class.

These findings illustrate the personal and political consequences of "internalized classism" (Russell, 1996). Distancing oneself from or denying associations with socially devalued groups (e.g., poor or working classes) has important implications not only for identity and self-concept but also for coalition building and political mobilization. It is this misidentification with so-called working-class concerns (e.g., welfare, unemployment insurance, food stamps, workplace safety) and affiliation with a universal middle class that policymakers appeal to when seeking support for initiatives that disproportionately benefit higher income groups.

Policymakers foster the perception of a normative middle class by blurring meaningful distinctions between the wealthy and other economic groups. Arguing on behalf of a "middle-class tax cut," then Speaker of the U.S. House of Representatives Newt Gingrich, for example, proposed including families with incomes up to $200,000 a year (Miller, 1995). His supporters accused critics of class warfare when they were unwilling to recognize earners at the upper end of this range as middle class. Similarly, the Bush administration tried to downplay significant differences in the economic impact of its stimulus package for families with annual earnings of $40,000 versus $400,000 by presenting all stockholders as the beneficiaries of their plan.

Media Myths and Distortions

Policymakers are not alone in framing the interests of the wealthy as mainstream concerns. Popular television programs and advertisements portray social class as a lifestyle choice whereby individuals buy status through the acquisition of material goods (Southerton, 2002; Steinhauer, 2005). Magazines and entertainment programs disclose where wealthy celebrities like to shop, what cosmetics they prefer, where they take their vacations, and what types of cars they drive (Seelye, 2005). The not-so-subtle message is that anyone can partake of the "good life" by making the "right" purchases.

Wealth is about power and access to resources, but media depictions of wealth do not present this reality. Recent reality programs featuring young people born into great wealth tend to neutralize the political implications of inequality. In the series *The Simple Life*, Paris Hilton of the Hilton hotel empire and Nicole Richie, daughter of performer Lionel Richie, gave up their lavish lifestyles and credit cards to live with working-class families and labor at blue-collar jobs. Each episode followed a predictable fish-out-of-water format, which involved the young women's designer clothing and "trashy" talk clashing with the homey lifestyles of their host family. In the second season of the program, the two women traveled across the country in a pink Airstream trailer, failing at their work assignments as maids, doughnut makers, and gas station attendants (e.g., sleeping in and arriving late, shirking their responsibilities, talking back to their bosses) and showing a fundamental lack of familiarity with basic aspects of daily living (e.g., driving, shopping at Wal-Mart, staying within a budget). Their disdain for physical labor and unfamiliarity with the dynamics of the workplace (e.g., Paris did not know how to use a punch-in time clock) were played for laughs. As observed by Sicha (2004),

> The jokes are always about how unfit they are for survival. Meanwhile, the less hilarious fact that they are pretending to be needy, while the trailer-park strangers on whose kindness they rely might actually be struggling to make ends meet, somehow gets swept under the Airstream. (¶2)

Watching these "poor little rich girls" struggle to master the basics of the "simple life" without any real-world repercussions for their incompetence (e.g., getting fired) trivializes the vast and significant differences in privilege and opportunity between social classes. In such media portrayals, inequality becomes little more than a clash of lifestyles. Any animosity viewers might feel toward those who never need to work for a living is neutralized by the reassuring message that "common folk" hold the moral upper hand. Even though the host families failed to "reform" their wealthy guests, the discipline and work ethic of the host families were presented as superior to the questionable values of the rich. Perhaps even more important, wealth was depicted as a personal characteristic rather than as a form of institutional power. As a host family member explained, "I've known of Paris's [great] granddaddy Conrad and Nicole's daddy . . . but they're just people, it doesn't matter how much money they have. You can live life whether you're rich or you're poor and just enjoy yourself" (quoted in Sicha, 2004, ¶13). The take-home message of all this is that the wealthy are just like the rest of us. Sicha (2004) noted that "Paris and Nicole emerge as an improbable vehicle for rehabilitation of the idle rich, in a non-threatening venue that's half vaudeville revue and half surrealist family-values intervention . . . the two semi-delinquents allow the rest of us to feel noble and poor" (¶14).

Meritocracy: A Truly Bipartisan Myth

The sting of class inequities is further blunted by the myth of *meritocracy*, or the belief that socioeconomic status is determined primarily by individual talent and ability and not by unearned advantage (e.g., inheritance, access to privileged social networks), discriminatory practices (e.g., bias in hiring), and group membership (e.g., class, gender, ethnicity; Bullock, 2004). Despite pervasive structural differences in access to resources (see chap. 4), "rags-to-riches" stories capture the public's attention and dominate political rhetoric. Where Republican discourse generally attempts to minimize the significance of class structure, Democratic rhetoric tends to focus on meritocracy. This perspective is apparent in former President Bill Clinton's speech to the Democratic Leadership Council (*Remarks to the Democratic Leadership Council*, 1993) in which he asserted that

> the American dream that we were all raised on is a simple but powerful one: If you work hard and play by the rules, you should

be given a chance to go as far as your God-given ability will take you. Throughout our history our party has been the fulcrum that allowed working people to lift themselves up into the middle class. And we know that if we're to be true to our historic mission we must be the party of the values and the interests of the middle class and, more importantly, the values and the interests of those who want to become part of the growing middle class and the American dream. (¶7)

Constructing class as an achieved rather than an ascribed status (Weber, 1998), such remarks portray the United States as an open economic system in which hard work prevails and the strongest, most capable candidate rises to the top. The belief that one can rise from humble beginnings to affluence is at the core of the American dream (Hochschild, 1995). A *New York Times* poll illustrated how cherished such beliefs are (Scott & Leonhardt, 2005). Of the respondents, 40% believed that opportunities for upward mobility had increased over the past 30 years, whereas 35% perceived no change. Only 23% of respondents believed that the chance of upward movement from one class to another had declined. It is the strong belief in the permeability of class boundaries, in conjunction with assumptions about equal access to valued resources such as quality education, that legitimates and helps to maintain the tremendous social and economic disparities that pervade our society.

Media profiles of "self-made" millionaires and self-help books that provide tips on how to "get rich quick!" make upward mobility seem attainable. As observed in a *Money* magazine Web article titled "Making It to the Top. It's Never Easy, but Getting Rich Is Still Being Done Every Day. All It Takes Is Leverage" (Futrelle, Birger, & Regnier, 2005), "The idea that anyone can make it here is so key to our national self-image it ought to be printed on the dollar bill" (¶1). The tacitly understood message is that those who don't "make it" are not hardworking or do not want to improve their financial position. President Clinton's reference to those who "want" to become part of the middle class reinforces the conviction that drive and personal willpower are central determinants of class position.

Socioeconomic data document the conclusion that moving up the economic ladder is more difficult than American dream rhetoric might lead one to believe (cf. Scott & Leonhardt, 2005). Studies examining class mobility have shown that many people remain in the same income quintile; a small percentage advance more than one quintile beyond where they started ("Meritocracy in America: Ever Higher Society, Ever Harder to Ascend," 2004). When gender, race, and educational attainment are taken into account, the likelihood of upward mobility for some groups becomes slim. Rank and Hirschl (2001) estimated that 30.7% of White men with 12 or more years of education will experience 1 year of poverty compared with a staggering 77.5% of Black women with similar educational backgrounds. Analysis of the likelihood of being affluent, defined by Rank and Hirschl as having an income 10 times the poverty threshold, revealed similar group differences. They found that two thirds of White men with 12 or more years of education will likely experience 1 year of affluence compared with 17.4% of their Black female counterparts and 4.6% of Black women with less than 12 years of education. Group inequities such as these challenge Geraldine Ferraro's assertion that "America is the land where dreams can come true for all of us" (*Geraldine Ferraro: 1984 Vice Presidential Nomination Acceptance Address*, 1984, ¶1).

Statistics on the distribution of income and wealth expose the gap between economic reality and the reassuring claim that "the promise of our country is that the rules are fair. If you work hard and play by the rules, you can earn your share of America's blessings" (*Geraldine Ferraro: 1984 Vice Presidential Nomination Acceptance Address*, 1984, ¶3). Income is now more concentrated among the very richest Americans than in all but 6 years since the mid-1930s (I. Shapiro, 2005). According to the CPBB (I. Shapiro, 2005), between 1979 and 2002 the average after tax income of the top 1% of the population grew by 111% (from $298,900 to $631,700), and the after tax income of the middle fifth of the population rose by only 15% (to $43,700). Over the same period, the poorest fifth of the population saw gains of only 5%, or $600. A *New York Times* analysis (Johnston, 2005a) showed just how rapidly the income gap is widening. Between 1950 and 1970, for every additional dollar made by the bottom 90% of earners, the top 1% of earners received an additional $162. The amount received by taxpayers at the top rose by a staggering additional $18,000 between 1990 and 2002. The top 10% of families also own approximately 90% of stocks and mutual funds, trusts, financial securities, and business equity and approximately 80% of nonresidential real estate (Wolff, 2004).

The effects of bifurcated income and wealth extend beyond the economic sphere to the political arena, where elites are able to control the political process and wield considerable influence over social policy. Great personal wealth and support from wealthy donors are increasingly necessary to win and remain in political office (Phillips, 2002). With 26.2% of the entire U.S. Congress believed to be millionaires, compared with just 1% of the U.S. voting population (Lioz & Cassady, 2003), there is little doubt that our elected officials do not share the same class background as the majority of their constituents. Commenting on the political implications of these trends for economic elites and the general public, Phillips (2002) noted the following:

> As wealth concentration grows . . . so has upper-bracket control of politics and its ability to shape its own preferment. The public has reason to be aroused, because the cost to ordinary Americans has been substantial—in reduced median income, in stagnant wages, in a diminished sense of community and commonweal, in fewer private and government services, and sometimes in poorer physical health and mental health. (p. xiv)

The wealthy are the chief beneficiaries of current government policy. Social psychological research provides considerable insight into how discourse about the American dream and belief in widespread economic opportunity contribute to the maintenance of political and economic advantage. Research on collective action consistently has found that members of low-status groups are less likely to engage in collective action when group boundaries are perceived as permeable, even if mobility is permitted for only a small token percentage (Wright, 2001; Wright, Taylor, & Moghaddam, 1990). Conversely, when boundaries are regarded as impassable, group members are more likely to act collectively than individually to improve their status. In this way, "American dream" rhetoric, with an emphasis on individual achievement and reward, discourages development of the strong interclass alliances needed to challenge the distribution of resources.

CHALLENGING CLASS WARFARE RHETORIC

The dominant rhetoric in our society that either denies class differences or exaggerates the potential for upward mobility contributes respectively to the relative silence about policies that benefit the wealthy and the multitude of voices that blame "welfare dependency" for a variety of our country's woes. This rhetoric renders the larger issues of discrimination, economic disparity, and the polarization of wealth invisible. Revealing these constructions is essential if the real mechanisms of class warfare—the policies and structures that maintain class privilege—are to be challenged. We offer several suggestions for increasing the probability of viewing the politics of class warfare through a critical lens.

First, wealth must be contextualized against the backdrop of poverty, or we risk allowing the growing concentration of wealth to remain unchecked. Neglecting the broader dynamics of inequality legitimates class warfare discourse by making the social conditions that create great wealth and crushing poverty invisible. Reporting income and poverty statistics together is one strategy for increasing awareness of how unequally resources are distributed and how some groups prosper at the expense of others. In 2004, the U.S. Census Bureau began reporting its annual figures on poverty, income, and health insurance together, making it easier to see the interrelationships among these variables. Descriptive statistics must be presented in ways that generate critical analysis. The use of annual income statistics to highlight gender inequity illustrates this point. The popular press reporting of women's earning power relative to men's (e.g., in 2004 women earned 77 cents for every dollar men earned) should be extended to other demographic categories (e.g., occupation; U.S. Census Bureau, 2005). Highlighting the disparity among the paychecks of executives, middle-class bureaucrats, public school teachers, nurses, assembly-line workers, and child-care providers can raise questions about the value ascribed to different types of labor and the fairness of these constructions.

Such a shift in our collective thinking also requires challenging the assumption that economic status is deserved. In the United States, there is a tendency, particularly among the White middle class, to attribute wealth to positive personal characteristics like hard work and ability and to attribute poverty to negative qualities like laziness and lack of intelligence (Cozzarelli et al., 2001; Feagin, 1975; Furnham, 2003; Kluegel & Smith, 1986). Structural causes of wealth such as inherited assets and privilege, family connections, and political influence tend to be minimized, as are structural causes of poverty like discrimination, low-quality schools, and low wages (Kluegel & Smith, 1986; K. B. Smith, 1985; K. B. Smith & Stone, 1989).

Attributional beliefs influence how economic "failure" and "success" are constructed as reflections of personal effort, not as reflections of social policy and politics that create and sustain wealth and poverty. The tendency to stereotype low-income groups as unmotivated, dependent "takers" is evident in a remark by Tom DeLay, the former majority leader of the U.S. House of Representatives. Democrats, he said, want "unlimited unemployment compensation so somebody could stay out of work for the rest of their lives and get unemployment compensation" (quoted in Hulse, 2003, p. A23). In another example, former President George H. W. Bush's statement, "If you don't feel something strongly you're not going to achieve" (quoted in Academy of Achievement, 1995, ¶9), situated "success" within the individual. This perspective is reinforced by annual listings of the richest people in the world and in books such as *Rich Dad, Poor Dad: What the Rich Teach Their Kids About Money That the Poor and Middle Class Do Not!* (Kiyosaki & Lechter, 1998). In the political struggle to control how resources are distributed, conservatives use the language of class warfare to activate particular attributions for wealth and poverty. This is a strategy to garner support for policies that benefit the rich and breed resentment for programs that direct resources to low-income groups.

"Welfare mothers" have been a favorite target of public hostility (Fiske, Xu, Cuddy, & Glick, 1999; Henry, Reyna, & Weiner, 2004; Rose, 2000) and have been presented as sexually promiscuous, living extravagantly off the welfare system, shunning marriage, and having children to increase the size of their monthly checks (Neubeck & Cazenave, 2001; Orloff, 2002; Quadagno, 1994; Vartanian & McNamara, 2004). This stereotype stands in sharp contrast to the reality of low-income women's lives (e.g., Banerjee, 2002; Holloway, Fuller, Rambaud, & Eggers-Pierola, 1997; Seccombe, 1999). Yet it is the sexist and racist mythology of the "welfare queen" that has dominated the cultural representation of welfare receipt. Former President Ronald Reagan capitalized on these stereotypes in an anecdote he repeatedly told about an African American woman who was arrested for welfare fraud:

> She has 80 names, 30 addresses, 12 Social Security cards and is collecting veteran's benefits on four non-existing deceased husbands. And she is collecting Social Security on her cards. She's got Medicaid, getting food stamps, and she is collecting welfare under each of her names. (quoted in Gilliam, 1999, p. 50)

Images of fraud, single motherhood, and out-of-control sexuality among African American women have remained firmly entrenched in the public's mind, serving as effective political weapons in the push to undermine welfare support.

By depicting poverty and welfare receipt as "Black" problems, the media helped legitimate the welfare queen stereotype (Avery & Peffley, 2003; Gilens, 1999; Quadagno, 1994) and fuel antiwelfare sentiment. This ultimately contributed to Clinton's successful 1992 bid for the presidency on his promise to "end welfare as we know it" and to the passage of the Personal Responsibility and Work Opportunity Reconciliation Act of 1996. Over the past few decades, news stories about poverty have come to be dominated by images of urban African Americans. Gilens (1999) examined three major news magazines and found that African Americans were pictured in 62% of stories about poverty, even though they made up only 29% of the poor at the time. Even when White recipients are profiled in news stories about welfare, they are less salient than Black welfare recipients. Gilliam (1999) had a group of White participants watch an 11-minute videotaped newscast that included a story about the impact of welfare reform on a hypothetical recipient named Rhonda. Across all conditions, the story remained constant; only Rhonda's ethnicity varied (White or Black). Nearly 80% of the respondents accurately recalled Rhonda's race when she was portrayed as Black, but less than 50% when she was portrayed as White. With racist beliefs among the strongest predictors of antiwelfare attitudes (Gilens, 1999), understanding how racism can be activated through visual imagery and political rhetoric is crucial.

Overvaluing of the wealthy and scapegoating of the poor have had profound consequences for social policy (Feagin, 1975; Kluegel & Smith, 1986). A study examining support for various welfare policies (Bullock, Williams, & Limbert, 2003) found that attributing poverty to individual deficiencies and wealth to individual strengths (e.g., skill, perseverance) predicted support for punitive welfare regulations (e.g., time limits, work requirements). Conversely, support for progressive policies (e.g., increased support for postsecondary education, extended child care, and medical benefits) was predicted by attributing poverty to structural causes, perceiving income inequality as unfair, and believing that wealth is undeserved and unearned. Similar findings have been reported regarding attitudes toward the elimination of the dividend tax, with warm feelings toward the wealthy and causal attributions of personal initiative emerging as the strongest predictors of support for eliminating the tax (Bullock & Fernald, 2005).

Such data make it clear that garnering support for a progressive tax system as well as affordable housing, real living wages, and access to quality child and medical care requires shifting attention toward the structural sources of poverty and wealth. This requires studying and challenging the dominant frames used to present these issues in political discourse and the media (Harper, 2003; Heider, 2004). We must carefully examine the following issues:

- how political beliefs interact with and are shaped by political rhetoric and the media (Iyengar, 1991; Nelson, Oxley, & Clawson, 1997; M. L. Roberts, Hite, & Bradley, 1994),
- what the public does and does not know about poverty and welfare reform (Catholic Campaign for Human Development, 2004; W. M. Epstein, 2004),
- what the public does and does not know about wealth and inequality (Hunt, 2004; Kluegel & Smith, 1986; McCall, 2003), and
- whose stories are told and whose stories are neglected and how these narratives challenge or maintain conservative conceptions of class warfare.

When an economic downturn followed problems within the dot-com industry, the mainstream media began to give increased attention to unemployment, but poverty and the poor continue to be largely invisible. Given the dearth of information about poverty in the popular press (Entman, 1995), it is unsurprising that poverty tends to be underestimated. Findings from a telephone survey of 1,008 respondents to a study commissioned by the Catholic Campaign for Human Development (2004) vividly illustrate this point. Although approximately 35 million people in the United States were poor at the time the study was conducted, the survey respondents grossly underestimated their numbers—the median estimate was only 1 million people.

In the wake of so-called welfare reform, the media have focused far more attention on the reduction of welfare caseloads than on the ongoing problem of poverty. Qualitative studies of "postreform" newspaper stories have revealed simplistic analyses that provide little discussion of poverty or the structural factors that perpetuate inequality in wealth and income (Bullock, Wyche, & Williams, 2001; Lens, 2002a, 2002b). Emphasis has been placed on the number of recipients no longer on the welfare rolls rather than on the low wages and continued poverty of former recipients (Bullock et al., 2001; Schram & Soss, 2001). Among the documented consequences of loss of welfare benefits uncovered by a longitudinal study of families in Illinois was a significant association between nonreceipt of welfare and an increase in the probability of criminal behavior (Lewis & Monte, 2004).

Not surprisingly, the vast majority of media articles have framed welfare as the problem rather than poverty, sexism, racism, or the distribution of resources (Bullock et al., 2001; Lens, 2002a, 2002b). Such findings document the belief that economic self-sufficiency is of paramount importance, that hard work pays off, and that the restrictive policies now in place are warranted. This perspective was evident in President George W. Bush's claim that welfare reform "put an end to the culture of dependency that welfare had created" (*President's Welfare Reform Package Strengthens Families*, 2003, ¶10).

The Bush administration continued to advocate for initiatives that further deepen the economic divide and jeopardize the already shaky financial well-being of poor and working-class families by extending the reduction of dividend taxes and pushing for the partial privatization of Social Security and stricter Temporary Assistance for Needy Families (TANF) policies. The political rhetoric and media framing of these initiatives undoubtedly influence public support for them. The president's plan for Social Security was to cut benefits to anyone born after 1950 with earnings of approximately $20,000 or higher (CBPP, 2005).

With respect to TANF reauthorization, his administration supported even tougher work requirements (40 hours per week rather than 30 to 35 hours), an increase in the percentage of recipients within a state who must be engaged in "work" activities (from 50% to 70%), and a stricter definition of "work" (e.g., disallowing some types of educational programs). These proposals tell us a great deal about the political climate. When simply questioning the differential impact of tax policies can be labeled "un-American," studying the beliefs that legitimate these policies takes on new urgency. Understanding the attitudes that lead the poor to be scrutinized while the rich are given the benefit of the doubt may prove to be one of our best tools in crafting effective campaigns against disparity-enhancing policies and mobilizing broad public support for them.

CONCLUDING THOUGHTS

The creation of a just economic system, one that is rooted in a genuine commitment to universal economic security, cannot be achieved without acknowledging the pervasiveness of class privilege. This privilege can be seen in discrimination in the tax code, the workplace, and the welfare system and in institutionalized power differences. Insistence that the United States is a classless society and a meritocracy ensures that we avoid engaging in a real national dialogue about class inequities, even as the distance between the rich and poor threatens to grow even wider.

The welfare reauthorization plan proposed by the current federal administration will bring harsher work requirements even as recently adopted tax policies are redistributing wealth upward. Proponents of these plans attempt to silence debate by branding those who oppose them as stirring up class warfare. Social psychological research and feminist analyses of power help us understand why this may be a successful tactic and how the politics of class rhetoric divert attention from the beneficiaries of disparity-enhancing policies (Limbert & Bullock, 2005).

In his second inaugural address in 1937, Franklin Delano Roosevelt (*Franklin D. Roosevelt: Second Inaugural Address*, n.d.) challenged the people of the United States to address the same inequities we face today when he said, "The test of our progress is not whether we add more to the abundance of those who have much; it is whether we provide enough for those who have too little" (¶29). Years from now, the details of current welfare reauthorization proposals and tax packages may be distant memories, but we suspect that we will still be working to dismantle the oppressive belief systems and power disparities that make such policies viable. This is one of our greatest challenges—changing the culture that allows these inequities to exist.

Forging a new social contract where caring, equity, and shared responsibility take center stage requires risk, dedication, and willingness to challenge the status quo. It also requires an ongoing attack on age-old assumptions about "deservingness" and the beliefs that legitimate our current "shareholder culture," in which even the most basic public services are regarded as individual responsibilities (Katz, 1989, 2001). Envisioning communities capable of taking on such challenges, Fine and Carney (2001) suggested that "we invite researchers and activists to recast our net so that responsibilities are distributed widely . . . and resist the temptation to locate this kind of social work squarely and painfully on the already burdened backs of women, particularly poor and working class women and women of color" (pp. 408–409). Breaking the silence around the politics of class and class warfare may be among the first steps.

Psychologists will need to extend our influence beyond the familiar arenas of the classroom and scholarly journals into local, state, and national policymaking spheres. U.S. social policies are not developed, debated, or implemented on a level playing field; policymakers and the media are not impartial observers. Nor are we. Psychologists cannot study social policies or the dominant cultural beliefs that support them outside the messy world of politics and power (Harper, 2003). Challenging the politics of greed—whether through progressive changes to the tax code, the creation of a just welfare system, or campaign finance reform—is critical to (re)conceptualizing our responsibility for one another personally and politically. It is also important that psychologists challenge the accrual of class privilege in our own lives and question the effects of individualism and other dominant cultural values on our willingness to ignore economic inequality. As Sloan (2003) noted, psychologists have not yet fully committed themselves to these challenges: "Given the sheer numbers of people in the world who are affected by poverty, it is striking how few psychologists in high-income countries are engaged directly in doing something about it" (p. 301). In the next chapter, we offer research and policy recommendations that move us in this direction.

6

Professional Activism for Social Change and Economic Justice

In this final chapter, we draw on the personal, psychological, and political analyses of poverty and inequality presented here to suggest strategies for promoting economic justice. Our discussion centers on aspects of class inequity that demand our immediate attention within both the field of psychology and society at large. Grounded in the thinking of feminist and other critical scholars, our recommendations are intended "to be of use" (Fine & Barreras, 2001, p. 175), to encourage activist research and teaching, and to energize psychologists and other allies to include issues of economic justice in their work. We offer suggestions in the spirit of generativity, with the understanding that transforming how psychologists think about, speak of, and study class issues will require the wisdom, creativity, and dedication of activists and scholars with diverse backgrounds. Many among us are committed to breaking down class-based hierarchies and barriers to resources. We can work together to achieve these goals.

DISRUPTING CLASSISM: AN ACTIVIST AGENDA FOR PSYCHOLOGISTS

A class-based activist agenda for psychologists begins with a careful analysis of how we approach economic (in)justice within our discipline, professional organizations, and relationships with colleagues. For example, although studies of the detrimental consequences of poverty point to the need for a universal health care system, equitable public school funding, and guaranteed income programs for low-wage earners, psychology has not taken the lead in advocating for these changes. Nor have psychologists denounced classism with the same vigor that has been brought to critical analyses of other forms of stigmatization and discrimination (Bullock, 1995; Lott, 2002a).

The American Psychological Association (APA), our primary professional organization, has been slow to embrace class-based issues and concerns. We noted in a previous chapter that APA's Council of Representatives passed a Resolution on Socioeconomic Status and Poverty in 2000 that called for increased research to describe the impact of economic disparity and classism, the development of educational curricula and training programs that are sensitive to the needs of socioeconomically diverse groups, and support for social policies that promote economic justice (APA, 2000; see Appendix). Yet, just 2 years later, the council voted to retire the Committee on Urban Initiatives, the only governance group that focused directly on class issues. In 2005, after considerable effort, a six-person, 2-year task force to study issues related to socioeconomic status was finally approved.

The need for the APA task force is illustrated by the exclusion of social class from important APA conferences and publications. For example, a new pamphlet from the Commission on Ethnic Minority Recruitment, Retention and Training (Trimble, Stevenson, & Worell, 2004) on how to infuse introductory psychology textbooks with diversity content deals with aging; culture, ethnicity, and race; disability; gender; and sexual orientation, but there is no mention of social class. Such an omission can convey the powerful message that class is not a valued dimension of human experience. Middle-class status is normalized, reinforcing the attitude that poor or working-class status is something that should be overcome or concealed. That social class is overlooked even among groups who are working to make psychology more inclusive underscores the need to bring it into a respected place within the multicultural literature. The appointment of an APA task force on socioeconomic status reflects a newly awakened class consciousness within psychology—an important step forward. A new task force formed by APA Divisions 9 and 35 will prepare resources on social class for inclusion in psychology curricula. It is our hope that these groups will be granted permanent governing status alongside the Committee on Women, the Committee on Ethnic Minority Affairs, and the Committee on Lesbian, Gay, and Bisexual Concerns.

Being a Psychologist and Being Middle Class

As we encourage our discipline to analyze and actively confront classism, we need to be cognizant of the relatively privileged, middle-class status that work as a psychologist affords. Graduate training and subsequent professional work in academic, clinical, or other applied settings distances most of us from experiencing the daily struggles of poverty and from being the targets of classist discrimination (Lott, 2002a). This is true even for those of us who grew up in poor or working-class families. Certainly, this is the case for both of the authors of this volume. It is also true of those among us who are minorities of color, who experience racism while earning substantial incomes and enjoying middle-class comforts and status. Our professional achievements and position may contribute to a reluctance to scrutinize the institutions from which we have benefited. The same questionable beliefs about meritocracy and upward mobility that dominate U.S. ideology may also influence how psychologists think about social class and economic disparity. Feminists and psychologists must acknowledge what the literature on beliefs demonstrates, a normative middle-class bias. Commenting on the need for feminists to understand class-based power differentials in the academic world, Reay (1999) observed the following:

> Once social class is addressed as an important concern for feminism then the psychology of class superiority and inferiority and the way in which it permeates relationships between women both in as well as outside the academy has to be recognized. . . . The ways in which hierarchy infuses the academy, including the perspectives of feminist academics, rarely make their way into feminist writing. . . . Yet many female academics have had the experience at conferences of talking to another woman who is constantly looking over her shoulder, trying to spot someone more prestigious to talk to. We women academics are caught up in the difficulties of escaping male frames of reference while colluding with male power. (p. 428)

One important challenge for feminist psychologists is to be mindful of how our judgments and behaviors are influenced by workplace structures and practices and how we actively participate in the reification of class boundaries by upholding biased value systems (e.g., the widespread assumptions that lecturers perform less valuable services than ladder-rank faculty, research institutions are more prestigious than teaching colleges, and research faculty should earn more than those who have higher teaching loads). Both of us who are writing this book, in the alternative routes we have taken to full-time positions at research-oriented universities, have experienced this type of elitism. The classism that pervades our professional interactions, especially in the form of unspoken ranking systems used to elevate or denigrate the professional "pedigree" of colleagues, must be addressed with the same intensity with which feminist psychologists have confronted sexism and racism in the workplace.

Research and Teaching in Psychology

Psychology will not become a more inclusive discipline until research and teaching are related to broad issues involving sociopolitical realities and change. Rejecting individuating theories of poverty and wealth is among the most fundamental but potentially transformative shifts psychologists can make. Although the culture of poverty hypothesis has been largely discredited, contemporary research continues to approach poverty as an individual rather than a social–structural problem (Marks, 1991; Wilson & Aponte, 1985). Commenting on the pervasiveness of this bias, O'Connor (2000) noted that

> the vast store of social scientific knowledge built up since the War on Poverty has focused far more heavily on the behavior, culture, and demographic characteristics of poor people than on the characteristics of the broader social structure, political culture, and economy that foster such high rates of poverty. (p. 548)

This has been the case in psychology, where deficit models have prevailed over structural approaches.

For example, the considerable attention paid to strengthening poor mothers' parenting skills and the assumed need for middle-class role models to teach work values to low-income adults are two illustrations of our field's tendency to pathologize the poor. Another example comes from the dominant approach taken to the homeless—which has been to create temporary shelters in which residents are often treated with disrespect and subjected to rules about personal behavior. Cosgrove and Flynn (2005) interviewed a small sample of homeless mothers in two shelters in the Northeast who were required to attend a parenting skills group. Many of the mothers said that the material presented did not meet their needs and often made them feel incompetent. A new approach, supported by the success of model programs (cf. Ziner, 2005b), first provides permanent safe, clean, and affordable housing and then offers support services. This approach has proved to be both more successful and less expensive and is what homeless people have been saying to policymakers and social scientists—they need housing first!

Psychologists have rallied against the most venomous classist attacks, most notably the flawed assertions of Herrnstein and Murray (1994), about the relationship between class and intelligence and between race and intelligence, but covert assumptions about individual responsibility for entering and exiting poverty go largely unchallenged. Nowhere is the need for structural analysis more evident than in research evaluating the welfare system. Such a shift would dramatically move evaluation of welfare reform from its current emphasis on the characteristics of the poor to an analysis of the institutional maintenance of poverty. Too many studies contrast the characteristics of "successful" welfare leavers with those who remain on assistance (e.g., Lichter & Jayakody, 2002; Zuckerman & Kalil, 2000). These studies say more about how to make welfare recipients fit the demands of the workplace than how structural factors (e.g., wages, benefits, education, neighborhood quality, racist discrimination, etc.) keep women and their families poor and how such factors might be changed (Riemer, 2001). Identification of the "best practices" for making women "work ready" appears to be the primary objective of welfare reform evaluation research rather than the development of effective strategies for preventing or reducing poverty. The fundamental question—"Best practices for whom?"—rarely surfaces in this discourse. Yet as Schram (2002) observed,

> "Best practices" suggests value neutrality and consensus about matters over which there is usually much conflict. . . . "Best practices" can become a way of instituting changes in treatment, intervention, or program administration while silencing consideration of the value conflicts associated with such changes. (p. 120)

Some feminist and other critical scholars have identified social scientists' complicit acceptance of dominant conceptions of welfare "dependency" and have argued for more analysis of racism, sexism, and classism within the welfare system and the workplace (Korteweg, 2003; Limbert & Bullock, 2005; Morgen & Maskovsky, 2003; Orloff, 2002; Steinitz & Mishler, 2001). These concerns have yet to be addressed by mainstream researchers. The high rates of mental health problems and violence among low-income women continue to be treated as individually experienced barriers to work instead of as manifestations of systemic inequality.

The paradigm shift that we are calling for requires replacing a fixation on welfare receipt and the work ethic and reproductive behaviors of low-income women with research that examines economic (in)security and its consequences for well-being within the context of growing income–wealth inequality and systemic classism, sexism, and racism (Morgen & Maskovsky, 2003; O'Connor, 2000). With respect to welfare policy, this means studying the consequences of punitive welfare policies for low-income families (Cherlin, Bogen, Quane, & Burton, 2002; Mink, 2001) as well as how these policies guarantee the availability of a low-wage labor force (Piven & Cloward, 1993). Such a labor force ensures profits for those who employ easily replaceable, unskilled, poorly trained, low-wage workers in a secondary labor market. We also need to look beyond statistics on the earnings of "welfare leavers" to examine the profits earned by corporate-run state welfare programs (Berkowitz, 2002). Is there also a relationship between "family cap" policies and "marriage promotion" programs and racist-inspired population control and compulsory heterosexuality (Neubeck & Cazenave, 2001)? The prevalence of stricter sanction policies in states with higher percentages of ethnic minority welfare recipients urge pursuit of such questions (Soss, Schram, Vartanian, & O'Brien, 2001).

Whom Are We Working For?

Psychologists need to (re)consider where we position our work in relation to dominant social institutions and whose interests are served by our research (Brodsky, 2001). The significance of positionality in shaping perspective, long a focal point of feminist scholarship (Graham, 2002; Harding, 1991; Hartsock, 1998; Pohlhaus, 2002), is evident in the discrepancy between the policymakers' claim that "welfare reform" is a success and low-income women's narratives of hardship within the new system and after exiting it (e.g., Bullock, Wyche, & Williams, 2001; Schram &

Soss, 2001). By focusing on declining caseloads rather than on questions of dignity, justice, and economic stability, "welfare reform" researchers affirm narrowly constructed measures of success and align themselves, perhaps inadvertently, with economically and socially privileged groups. Describing this dilemma, Steinitz and Mishler (2001) observed that

> once the official definition of the problem is accepted as the primary research frame and the norms of neutrality and technical objectivity are assumed for analyses and presentations of data, the researcher gives up the option of directly expressing her personal concerns or allying herself with her subjects. (p. 164)

A liberatory psychology will be grounded in the needs and concerns of oppressed groups, not funding agencies, policymakers, or other elites (Moane, 2003). This requires replacing so-called neutral and top-down approaches to knowledge with research that is contextually grounded, openly political, and allied with the struggles of oppressed groups (Schram, 2002). Reconceptualizing the relationship between social science research and human welfare, Schram proposed that

> research is not something that provides definitive answers to what social welfare policy ought to look like as much as it becomes another useful device for leveraging political change. Under these conditions, researchers perform an underlaborer's role, but it is an underlaborer for those struggling to overcome the oppressions of the existing social order. And research helps perform this role by providing politically contingent, historically contextualized, socially bounded knowledge that can help strengthen efforts for social change . . . it is situated, partial, and interested knowledge tied to political struggle and efforts to change social conditions. (p. 112)

Such an approach is compatible with the production of empirically based knowledge that is objectively verifiable and positions the expertise and experiences of low-income people at the core of how we study welfare reform and its consequences. We need to examine the impact of mandatory "work first" policies on self-respect, family well-being, pressure to participate in illegal activities, and the academic and social lives of children. Do women who look for work meet with discrimination after having been Temporary Assistance for Needy Families (TANF) recipients? This question was the subject of dissertation research by Jacob (2005), who found that former TANF recipients and Black job applicants were significantly less likely to be recommended for an administrative assistant position (for which they were qualified) than for a lower paying cashier position. Documenting the racism and classism that follows women from the welfare system into the workforce is essential to understanding the differential impact of allegedly neutral reform policies and labor practices.

The experiences of low-income women who report debasing, disrespectful, and humiliating responses to their efforts to obtain the assistance of medical personnel, educators, social workers, and psychologists need to be validated (Bartle & Segura, 2003; Bullock, Downing, & Limbert, 2004; Campbell & Raja, 2005; Gooden, 1998; Price, Desmond, Snyder, & Kimmel, 1988). Discriminatory or neglectful treatment may have life-or-death consequences. Some California welfare recipients, for example, have described receiving insufficient information from caseworkers about mental health and domestic violence services and, in some instances, being discouraged from seeking assistance (Bartle & Segura, 2003). Other research has revealed racist bias in client–caseworker interactions, with Black welfare recipients reporting significantly less discretionary assistance (e.g., transportation) and support for pursuing formal education than White recipients (Gooden, 1998). Discrimination in these situations reflects multiple oppressions and must be viewed through an intersectional lens (McCall, 2005; A. J. Stewart & McDermott, 2004) that takes into account the effects of complex intersecting factors, including limited English proficiency and religious beliefs. Those who have been absent from the analyses of psychologists must be included, and we need to compare responses to low-income men with those to women (Cozzarelli, Tagler, & Wilkinson, 2002; Fine & Weis, 1998).

The critical approach we are advocating situates poverty in a broader context of inequality, power, and intergroup relations instead of being focused on the behaviors and choices of poor or working-class persons. Mary Robinson, the former president of Ireland, urged an even broader context, that of human rights, in noting that such rights deal with more than "shielding people from violence and political despots . . . [and also includes] preventing hunger, homelessness, and disease" (quoted in Stambor, 2005, p. 26). Class privilege, not disadvantage, becomes the focal point, shifting attention toward those who benefit from inequality, the attitudes and beliefs that justify economic disparity, and the impact of social location on interpersonal and institutional treatment. Put simply, inequality and class stop being solely about the poor; they include the beneficiaries of economic disparity.

This approach can, for example, guide studies that examine the relationship between social class and health and medical care. In terms of health outcomes, the poor bear the brunt of economic inequality and the rich reap the rewards, benefiting from the expertise of leading physicians; access to state-of-the-art procedures; and disposable income to pay for preventive measures, rehabilitative services, and other health-related expenses (Robert, 1999; Scott, 2005). Inequality has broad and significant consequences. Residents of egalitarian societies live longer than residents of the wealthiest societies (Belle & Doucet, 2003), and in the United States, "income inequality and poverty together could account for about one-quarter of the state variations in mortality" (Kawachi & Kennedy, 1999, p. 217). Such findings should encourage us to look beyond individual risk factors to the social, cultural, and political pathways through which inequality operates in life expectancies. As Belle and Doucet (2003) noted,

> The deadly effects of income inequality appear to be mediated by the stresses of life in a winner-take-all economy, losses in social cohesion and trust, and the skewing of social policies in favor of the wealthy at the expense of the poor and the middle class. (p. 105)

To effectively interrupt the status quo of inequality, collective action is necessary. Thus, psychologists need to investigate the conditions that facilitate such action. In the wake of welfare reform and the unraveling of other safety net programs, political action by low-income groups is gaining momentum. There have been demonstrations against marriage-promotion proposals and protests against proposed cuts to child-care spending. An analysis by Reese and Ramirez (2002) of the fight to restore welfare benefits to immigrants in California highlighted the transformative potential of strong coalitions. Guishard et al. (2005) have described the work of a parent group in New York City working actively for educational equity in collaboration with their teenage children and academic psychologists. Their work is an example of participatory action research, a strategy for consultation and organizing within low-income communities. Increasing the agency and power of low-income people is the surest way to influence social policy and to change the culture of help-giving agencies.

The Need for Collective Action

Social psychologists have identified a number of factors that influence collective action; these include identifying with the marginalized group, perceived permeability of group boundaries, and beliefs about the legitimacy of structured inequities (Kelly & Breinlinger, 1996). Beyond personal characteristics (attitudes and beliefs), we must examine particular contexts and the available, visible, and organizational structures and movements that contribute to classism (Lott & Webster, in press). Proximity to welfare rights organizations and a strong presence (e.g., flyers, presentations) in the places low-income women frequent are among the most important facilitators of political mobilization among them (Bullock et al., 2004). Identifying the situational forces that stimulate or stall collective action is crucial, as is examining how social policies affect civic engagement and create arenas for political action (Mettler & Soss, 2004). We can study labor-based activism across contexts, including initiatives by organized labor and the development of less formal movements on college campuses. Attention must also be given to the strategies that powerful groups use to attract those with less power to their political causes and to prevent the formation of strong oppositional coalitions capable of challenging gross inequities (Apfelbaum, 1999; Hurtado, 1996).

These recommendations are grounded in our desire to work effectively and collaboratively with low-income groups, community agencies, and other researchers (Brodsky, 2001; Brodsky et al., 2004; Reid & Vianna, 2001). They require the skillful use of diverse methodologies and other tools for promoting social change (Camic, Rhodes, & Yardley, 2003; Tolman & Brydon-Miller, 2001). Nurturing and encouraging justice-oriented researchers requires restructuring graduate training to include participatory and field research in the honored tradition of Kurt Lewin's (1946) action research, in which psychologists are directly engaged with communities and with low-income individuals and families in social change efforts (Fine et al., 2003; McIntyre, 2000). This means supporting students who wish to pursue this kind of dissertation work, teaching appropriate methodology courses, and incorporating such research in psychology's definitions of good empirical science.

Undergraduate service learning programs have grown tremendously, emerging as an invaluable way to immerse students in social justice learning and advocacy (Leonard, 2004). In addition to supporting stand-alone service learning courses, we must develop innovative strategies for connecting classroom learning with community-based learning and action. Heather Bullock, for example, offers an optional service-based practicum in conjunction with an upper division lecture course on poverty and social class that gives students the opportunity to intern with local antipoverty organizations. Similar programs need to find their way into graduate training. Graduate students can be encouraged to pursue internships within the many sites where injustices routinely occur and successful advocacy transforms communities: schools, social service agencies, homeless shelters, prisons, medical centers, hospital emergency rooms, unemployment offices, and factories. These are important sites for research, where psychologists can put their skills to use by conducting needs assessments, identifying attitudinal and structural barriers to service provision, and examining the personal and community consequences of underemployment and unemployment, low wages, and poverty. Such efforts must be augmented by ensuring that action-oriented scholarship (e.g., policy briefs, community evaluations) is evaluated fairly and respectfully in tenure and other personnel reviews in academe as well as in grant proposals for funded research.

Social class will not become a central focus in graduate or undergraduate education in psychology or other university programs without broad-based support from colleagues. Departments must commit to infusing material about social class into required courses, supporting advanced courses that explore class-based concerns (e.g., the social psychology of social justice, the psychology of social class and poverty), and sponsoring working-class studies courses. Creating affirming environments for first-generation college students and low-income students in our classrooms by educating others about class inequities and sharing information about own class backgrounds is also critical, as is supporting working-class people on campus in their bids for higher wages (Jones, 2003).

Improving the climate of college classrooms for poor and working-class students may aid in retention but does not address the barriers that prevent college attendance. In addition to supporting tuition waivers and other forms of financial support for low-income students, psychologists must join forces with other educators to develop strategies to overcome the discrimination faced by low-income parents and their children in the public schools. Disrespect from teachers and low expectations regarding their abilities deter young people from staying in school or pursuing further educational opportunities (Lott, 2001; Lott & Rogers, 2005). We have personally experienced the lowered academic expectations that come with poor and working-class status. Crumbling public schools also send a powerful message about the lack of support for students in low-income neighborhoods. Analyzing the impact of attending run-down schools, Fine, Burns, Payne, and Torre (2004) noted,

> Poor and working-class youth of color are *reading* these conditions of their schools as evidence of their social disposability and evidence of public betrayal. . . . Like children who learn to love in homes scarred by violence, these young women and men are being asked to learn in contexts of humiliation, betrayal and disrespect. (p. 2194)

Improving the conditions in which poor children learn will require school finance reform; redistricting; and increased awareness of bias in teaching, teaching materials, and tests. These need to be among our highest priorities as psychologists committed to enhancing human welfare. As we advocate for these changes, we must continue building an arsenal of evidence that makes the urgency of our recommendations undeniable.

These suggestions are certainly not cost free. A progressive agenda requires rethinking the methodologies we use, the issues we investigate, and the curricula we teach. In other words, we must change how we go about our business. For some researchers, this will include turning down grant opportunities that equate "successful" reform with recipient compliance and behavior modification; for others this will mean fewer publications in mainstream journals; and for still others, it will require recognition of class privilege in their research circles and everyday interactions. Relative to what we stand to gain, these may be small costs, particularly in light of the policy struggles that lie before us.

HUMAN WELFARE AND ECONOMIC JUSTICE: A POLICY TO-DO LIST

Policy changes over the past several decades have gutted the safety net for millions of low-income families, leading some poverty scholars to conclude that our nation has shifted from waging a "war on poverty" to a "war against the poor" (Katz, 1989). The redistribution of income and wealth upward has further amplified the effects of insufficient welfare and health care policies, increasing the vulnerability of already fragile families. In this era of devolution and retrenchment, working against inequality requires strong interclass alliances. Psychologists have an important role to play in fostering such alliances and in developing a strong policy agenda. Although we recognize that the creation of a more just society is tied to a broad set of interrelated environmental, labor, and economic policies and practices, we focus here on changes to federal and state policies that would provide immediate benefits to low-income women and their families and to us all.

Real Welfare Reform

It is crucial that TANF be replaced with new legislation that focuses on ways that the federal government can assist low-income families in becoming financially secure and permanently exiting a life of poverty. The creation of just antipoverty programs requires substantive policy changes as well as fundamental philosophical shifts in welfare policy. For example, ending welfare's status as an entitlement program has jeopardized the economic security of all women by making assistance conditional rather than guaranteed. Antipoverty programs are the responsibility of governments, not private foundations or charitable organizations. In practical terms, this means removing the caps placed on federal funding for welfare programs and providing states with guaranteed support for recipients. It also means using funding formulas that are based on current need.

To achieve the objective of interrupting the oppression of poverty, U.S. welfare policy needs to be guided by a structural approach to program development and implementation. The amelioration of poverty and its root causes is noticeably absent from TANF's stated goals:

(1) provide assistance to needy families so that children may be cared for in their own homes or in the homes of relatives; (2) end the

dependence of needy parents on government benefits by promoting job preparation, work, and marriage; (3) prevent and reduce the incidence of out-of-wedlock pregnancies and establish annual numerical goals for preventing and reducing the incidence of these pregnancies; and (4) encourage the formation and maintenance of two-parent families. (Personal Responsibility and Work Opportunity Reconciliation Act of 1996, p. 2113)

These goals illustrate TANF's value-biased emphasis on women's marital status and parenting decisions.

These same priorities have dominated reauthorization proposals despite limited empirical evidence that "legislating marriage" will reduce poverty (Lind, 2004; Seefeldt & Smock, 2004; Wells & Baca Zinn, 2004). The Deficit Reduction Act of 2005, which reauthorized the TANF program through 2010, allocated $150 million annually for the promotion of "healthy marriages" and "responsible fatherhood." Research has shown that these funds would be better spent helping low-income women care for themselves and their families, an objective that is rarely articulated in the dominant discourse of "reform."

Developing new goals for reform will require debunking racist stereotypes about the weak work ethic and exaggerated sexuality of women of color (Neubeck & Cazenave, 2001; Quadagno, 1994), sexist stereotypes regarding the "dangers" of single motherhood (Orloff, 2002; Vartanian & McNamara, 2004), and classist beliefs about the moral and intellectual inferiority of the poor (Furnham, 2003; Kluegel & Smith, 1986). Discrediting such myths is crucial to the adoption of structurally oriented welfare policies. As described earlier in this chapter, psychologists can help in this endeavor by doing some of the needed research.

Welfare programs can be geared toward providing families with the resources they need to become financially secure—health care, transportation, housing, nutritious food, vocational training or other education opportunities, and quality child care (Rice, 2001). Currently, applicants are often humiliated and told to seek help from family or friends, diverted from completing formal applications, sanctioned with full or partial benefit reductions for small infractions, and threatened with being removed from the welfare rolls when time limits are met regardless of need (Hall & Strege-Flora, 2002; Hancock, 2002; Wiley, 2002). These common practices, coupled with "work-first" requirements, are guided by the belief that welfare recipients need discipline more than living wages, education, or other support services. Research has shown that the most disadvantaged families are hardest hit by these policies (Cherlin et al., 2002; Hasenfeld, Ghose, & Larson, 2004; Seefeldt & Orzol, 2004).

A growing body of evidence has raised serious questions about the effectiveness of work-first initiatives and other punitive reforms (Cintron-Velez, 2002; Delgado, 2002; Riemer, 2001; Schorr, 2001). For example, higher education, not workfare, has been found to be a better pathway to higher wages and job security (McCrate & Smith, 1998; Shaw, 2004). Nevertheless, mandated work remains at the core of TANF reauthorization. In the most recent legislation, required work participation rates remain unchanged at 50% for all families and 90% for two-parent families, but changes to how the caseload reduction credit is calculated will result in stricter enforcement of these requirements. Under the 1996 law, a "caseload reduction credit" allowed states to adjust their required participation rates downward by deducting "one percentage point for each percentage-point decline in the state's TANF caseload since 1995" (Parrott et al., 2006, p. 8). Under the Deficit Reduction Act, the credit is now based on caseload declines after 2005. With minimal or no decline in TANF caseloads since 2005, many states will see their caseload reduction credit disappear or decline significantly, resulting in new, higher work participation requirements (Legislative Analyst's Office, 2006). With TANF now assisting "fewer than half of all families with children who qualify" (Parrott et al., 2006, p. 1), few states will be able to reduce their caseloads below 2005 levels without limiting access to assistance. In the quest to meet stricter work participation rates, more recipients will be pushed into dead-end work with no consideration of the quality of work experiences or the ability of the labor market to integrate these workers. Once again, the most basic tenets of access, opportunity, and economic mobility will likely be ignored.

Punitive reforms serve to further institutionalize poverty. These include time limits, "family cap" policies, sanctions, restricted access to higher education, and work requirements. Instead, we should advocate increasing valued resources such as education, food, housing, and health care, making them accessible to all, poor and working-class groups.

Access to Education

Issues of educational access and equity must be addressed at all levels and be viewed as a high priority. Analyses of the economic status of students enrolled at 4-year colleges have highlighted this need. Fifty percent of undergraduates at top-tier universities are from families in the highest earning quintile, compared with only 11% from the lowest earning quintile (Bowen, Kurzweil, & Tobin, 2005). A mere 3% are from the poorest quartile and are also first-generation college students (Bowen et al., 2005).

Statistics such as these, and those discussed in chapter 4, clearly illustrate the economic barriers to higher education (e.g., Bowen et al., 2005; Quinn, 2003). Such data must be shared with legislators to encourage them to provide more direct support (not loans) for higher education for low-income students, similar to the post–World War II GI Bill. Congress must increase funding for Pell grants. When the program began in 1972, grants were large enough to cover 84% of the fixed costs at 4-year public institutions; now they cover half as much (Quinn, 2003).

In most states, school districts are funded inequitably (Augenblick, Myers, & Anderson, 1997; Howell & Miller, 1997; Terman & Behrman, 1997). Making school financing fair will require more than redistributing property taxes. Expenditures must be adjusted to reflect variability in student needs (e.g., bilingual education, special education classes) and the costs associated with educational resources in different areas ("Appendix B: Equity Considerations in Funding Urban Schools," 1997).

The costs of salaries, supplies, and space vary regionally, and these differences must be factored into funding formulas.

Equity for children in public schools should be an issue that is raised with every candidate for public office in local, state, and federal elections. State education departments need to hold school districts accountable for high drop-out rates as well as for the high numbers of low-income minority students classified as in need of special education (Grossman, 1998; National Center for Education Statistics, 2004). In the current political climate, *accountability* has come to mean punishing poorly performing schools by reducing their funding. We doubt this is an effective way to strengthen already-struggling communities. Instead, such school districts need increased resources and creative strategies to address the correlates of poor academic performance (such as poor nutrition, insufficient books, and disrespectful educators). School personnel need to learn more about cultural and racist testing practices and about sources of classist and racist bias in the classroom.

Psychological research can inform these and other advocacy efforts, such as efforts for early education and child-care programs. A growing body of research has made it clear that early education programs like Early Head Start and Head Start and high-quality child-care programs are associated with improved school readiness, cognitive and socioemotional development, and reduced delinquency and grade retention (Magnuson & Waldfogel, 2005; Reynolds, Temple, & Ou, 2003; Zigler & Styfco, 2003). Twelve million preschoolers, including 6 million infants and toddlers, attend child-care programs, but this figure represents only half of all eligible families. Lack of child-care subsidies for low-income families is a major barrier to access, resulting in only one in seven children who are eligible for child-care assistance receiving it (Children's Defense Fund [CDF], 2005b). Needy families are put on waiting lists or turned away entirely because of insufficient funding. To deal with this crisis, many states have established income limits that disqualify needy low-income families. According to the CDF, a family earning $25,000 a year would not qualify for assistance in over one-third of states (CDF, 2005b).

The situation for Head Start is also dire, with only half of all eligible preschool-age children participating in the program during fiscal year 2003 (CDF, 2005a). Early Head Start, which supports low-income families with children younger than 3 years and pregnant women, serves less than 3% of eligible infants and toddlers (CDF, 2005a).

In addition to protecting these programs from ongoing budgetary attacks, state legislators must be encouraged to lower income eligibility rules, waive copayments for families within 250% of federal poverty thresholds, update maximum state reimbursement rates so providers will be paid at market value for their services, and create state child-care tax provisions for parents (CDF, 2004). Ultimately, a program of federally funded universal preschool must replace the current fragmented and means-tested early childhood education programs. In some states, such as Georgia, New York, and California, universal preschool initiatives are gaining political momentum.

End Hunger in the United States

Congress must substantially increase its support for food assistance and insist that states simplify access to food stamps. Hunger and food insecurity continue to be significant problems. According to the U.S. Department of Agriculture (USDA, 2004b), 36.3 million people lived in hungry or food-insecure households in 2003, including 23 million adults (10.8% of all adults) and 13.3 million children (18.2% of all children). Yet, in 2002, only 54% of those eligible for food stamps received them (USDA, 2004a). Because food stamps are a critical source of support for low-income and working-class families (including one of our own families when growing up), national, state, and local changes are needed to improve access.

States can improve food stamp participation substantially by making sure that potential recipients are not diverted from completing applications, providing evening and weekend hours to accommodate applicants who are unavailable during regular daytime hours, and allowing families to apply at the same sites where they apply for other benefits (Food

Research and Action Center [FRAC], 2002). Applications, which average 12 pages in length but are as long as 18 pages in some states, can certainly be shortened (FRAC, 2002). Outreach efforts can be intensified to reach those who are unaware of their eligibility for benefits. In addition, food chains need to be encouraged to welcome those who use food stamps. In such an effort in Rhode Island as part of an advocacy group, Bernice Lott experienced initial strong disapproval of the group's customer-education efforts by a store manager, followed by eventual agreement on the part of higher management. Food stamp and TANF eligibility must be restored to those with felony drug convictions. It is estimated that nationally, 92,000 women are banned from receiving much-needed food assistance because of this punitive regulation and that as a consequence, 135,000 children are affected (FRAC, 2002). Other regulations also impede access to food stamps for needy families. For example, many states have 3-month reapplication requirements and require monthly income update check-ins (FRAC, 2002).

We can encourage state legislatures to mandate breakfast programs in all of their school districts. Recent success in this regard can encourage even more improvements. During the 2003–2004 school year, 79.4% of schools that served school lunch also operated school breakfast programs, up from 78.3% in 2002–2003 (FRAC, 2004). More children are now participating in the program. According to FRAC (2004), "for every 100 low-income children eating free or reduced-price school lunch, 43.1 also participate in the breakfast program" (p. v). This figure, up from 42.3 during the 2002–2003 school year, is the largest improvement in this ratio in a decade (FRAC, 2004).

State outreach campaigns and local antihunger initiatives have increased participation rates, but accessibility remains a major concern. For every 100 students receiving free or reduced-price school lunches, more than 50 do not receive a free school breakfast (FRAC, 2004). An estimated 2 million more eligible children must be reached (FRAC, 2004). The Child Nutrition and WIC Reauthorization Act of 2004 (P.L. 108-265) seeks to improve accessibility by making homeless, migrant, and runaway children automatically eligible for free school meals and by requiring schools to accept children in food stamp households as eligible for free school meals, which will reduce the need for parents to file additional application materials (FRAC, 2004).

The well-documented relationship between eating a nutritious breakfast, good health, and learning (e.g., Bhattacharya, Currie, & Haider, 2004; Murphy, Pagano, et al., 1998; Worobey & Worobey, 1999) can be used to support the adoption of a universal school breakfast program. Universal access is the best way to reduce the stigma of means-tested programs and guarantee that all school children start their day ready to learn. To ensure that low-income children have access to nutritious meals when school is out of session, support for after school programs and the Summer Food Service Program must also be increased.

Universal Access to Health Care

We urgently need legislation for a single-payer universal health care system that will be equivalent to "Medicare for all." As Krugman (2005c) noted, "America already has a highly successful, popular single-payer program, albeit only for the elderly" (p. A17). In the richest nation in the world, access to medical care has become a privilege that too many cannot afford. More than 45 million people are without health insurance (U.S. Census Bureau, 2005), and millions more are underinsured (Schoen, Doty, Collins, & Holmgren, 2005). Medical bills are bankrupting middle-class families (Himmelstein, Warren, Thorne, & Woolhandler, 2005). The price we pay as the only industrialized country that does not guarantee health care to its citizens is a high one in terms of both expense and limited access. In a 2003 poll by the Pew Charitable Trusts (2003), 26% of U.S. respondents reported not having had enough money to pay for family health care during the previous year compared with only 13% of Canadians, 12% of Italians, and 5% of the French. With 72% of Americans favoring universal government-guaranteed health insurance, there is clearly support for such structural change (Krugman, 2005c).

Some influential physicians' group, including the Physicians' Working Group for Single-Payer National Health Insurance (2003) and the American Medical Student Association (Chua, 2006), have been calling for such federal legislation. U.S. Representative John Conyers (a Democrat from Michigan) has introduced such a bill into Congress. Under the U.S. National Health Insurance Act (2005), or the Expanded and Improved Medicare for All Act, as it is also known, all residents of the United States would be covered for health care and medications, with parity for mental health services. The latter is something that APA has long supported and lobbied for in Congress, yet APA has not actively supported such progressive legislation as the Conyers bill, drafted with the help of a group of physicians. Doing so would act on the suggestion of former APA president Norine Johnson (2003) that APA policy statements be "used as tools to promote increased health care access" (p. 675).

In recent years, HMOs have proliferated because they presumably control medical expenses and thereby increase corporate profits. As the increased costs and inequities of health care have indicated, HMOs are not a solution to the national health care crisis in the United States. It is of considerable interest that a Gallup poll conducted in May 2005 (cf. "Whom Do You Trust?," 2005) found that HMOs were trusted the least among a number of U.S. institutions (including the military, banks, TV news, etc.). Only 7% of respondents said they trusted HMOs a great deal, and 37% said they trusted them very little to not at all. Opponents of universal health care initiatives will undoubtedly try to capitalize on public mistrust of HMOs by blurring meaningful distinctions between these programs, universal health care plans, and "socialized medicine." As psychologists work to mobilize support for single-payer plans, we must dedicate significant resources to educating the public about misleading language.

Improving access and quality of care will require adopting comprehensive long- and short-term goals. Until efforts to achieve universal health care succeed, Medicaid, the primary medical safety net for low-income adults and families, must also be protected from further budget cuts. State reductions in the scope of covered services and increased out-of-pocket expenses (e.g., copayments, deductibles) are jeopardizing the health of the poor and the quality of care they receive (Ku & Broaddus, 2005). In fiscal year (FY) 2003, 17 states raised or imposed new Medicaid copayments; in FY 2004, 20 states did so; and in FY 2005, 8 states increased copayments. For FY 2006, 13 states adopted new or higher copayments (Kaiser Commission on Medicaid and the Uninsured, 2005). Many low-income women and members of their families, unable to make these payments, will be forced to forgo necessary medical treatment. Psychologists must help defeat state initiatives that place an increasing share of sky-high medical expenses on Medicaid recipients, remaining mindful that strengthening Medicaid alone will not eliminate deeply entrenched race and class disparities in care. As Cornelius (2003) explained,

> We will never fairly address the health care needs of the "other America" unless we link them to our plight. By scrapping the private health insurance and Medicare plan and developing a uniform national health insurance plan, the poor and the non-poor tie their fates and successes to each other. (p. 18)

What is true of our school systems is also true of medical care: separate is not equal.

In this chapter, we have made a number of policy recommendations that we strongly believe in. No one can offer a complete and permanent policy agenda to combat classism and secure social justice for all. As Schram (2002) noted, "Social justice itself is something that must be continually redefined, as an ever-reconsidered, never fully realized socially desired state" (p. 112). Thus, the recommendations we have outlined here cannot be fully realized without accompanying changes to the minimum wage and ultimately support for self-sufficiency wages (Pearce, 2002a), the adoption of caregivers' wages for those who work in the home (Albeda, 2002), transportation vouchers for low-income families, and improved housing subsidies and quality housing for low-income people (Rollins, Saris, & Johnston-Robledo, 2001). It is equally crucial that we redress tax policies that redistribute income and wealth upward (see chap. 4).

FINAL THOUGHTS

In closing, we take one final opportunity to restate our primary objective—using our work and skills as psychologists to improve the personal and economic well-being of low-income women and families. Findings from a participatory action research project in which low-income women were asked what constitutes a good quality of life (Collins, 2005) offered direct insights into what is needed. Many of the factors the women identified are similar to what many of us hope for, regardless of our class status: strong relationships with friends and family, love, happiness, self-esteem, good health, savings, a secure job, a vacation, and the ability to pursue our dreams and help others in need. Yet, other factors that they associated with the "good life" are apt to be less salient or pressing to middle-class readers of this book: fresh water and enough to eat, full cupboards, and safe housing. Commonly cited threats to the "good life" included stress, worry, poor health, inadequate housing, inability to afford help, and the fear that children were headed in a bad direction. Classism was identified as a major source of stress, with one informant describing life on public assistance as "living under a giant microscope" (Collins, 2005, p. 18).

Such findings bring our primary reasons for writing this book into sharp focus: to bring the values of feminist psychology to bear on pressing national issues of inequality and to urge feminist psychologists to extend our thinking from gender, race, ethnicity, sexual orientation, and disability to social class. We have documented the many ways that our nation is failing its poorest, most vulnerable residents, women and their families. As the gap between the rich and poor widens and a growing portion of our population struggles for survival, let alone the attainment of the good life, another much smaller group, the very wealthiest among us, reaps the fruits of their labor.

Feminist psychologists and the discipline of psychology have much to offer in terms of bringing the inequities of classism and its intersections with racism and sexism to the forefront of public consciousness. We wholeheartedly second Fine's (2002) call "to resurrect a critical feminist psychology that reveals the long arm of the State and economic, racial, and gender arrangements in the everyday lives of women, men, and children" (p. 11). Many fundamental questions of class and power remain largely unexamined by psychologists: How is class privilege experienced, justified, and manifested on a daily basis? How are dominant cultural messages about class status and mobility interpreted and reinterpreted by different socioeconomic groups? How are strong interclass alliances fostered? What would a just welfare system look like? What can be done to weaken the structural forces that keep so many among us poor?

As psychologists, we wish to entrust the task of developing a progressive policy agenda to our colleagues in social services, public schools, community agencies, nonprofit organizations, academe, and state and national legislatures. We envision a psychology that is committed to conceptualizing class advantage and economic disparity as issues of power and oppression for which we are all responsible. Adopting such an approach may transform the field of psychology, resulting in new conceptualizations of human welfare, responsibility, and social justice, and help to transform our society.

Resolution on Poverty and Socioeconomic Status

Adopted by the American Psychological Association, August 6, 2000

WHEREAS, the income gap between the poor and the rich has continued to increase, with the average income of the poorest fifth of the population down 6% and the average income of the top fifth up 30% over the past 20 years (Bernstein, McNichol, Mishel, & Zahradnik, 2000);

WHEREAS, the poverty rate in the United States is higher now than in nearly all years of the 1970s, child poverty (at 18.9% in 1998, representing 13.5 million children) continues to be higher here than in most other industrialized nations, and the proportion of the population living below the poverty line in 1998 was 12.7% (representing 34.5 million people) (Center on Budget and Policy Priorities, 1999; U.S. Census Bureau, 1999);

WHEREAS, although Whites represented the largest single group among the poor in 1998, ethnic groups were overrepresented, with 26.1% of African Americans, 25.6% of Hispanics, 12.5% of Asians and Pacific Islanders, and 31% of American Indians on reservations living in poverty (National Congress of American Indians, 2000; U.S. Census Bureau, 1999), compared with the 8.2% of Whites who were poor;

WHEREAS, families* with a female head of household had a poverty rate of 29.9% in 1998 and comprised the majority of poor families (U.S. Census Bureau, 1999);

WHEREAS, the Task Force on Women, Poverty, and Public Assistance of the APA Society of the Psychology of Women (Division 35) has documented from the social sciences research literature the root causes of poverty and its impact for poor women, children, and their families, and called for a more effective public policy founded on this research base (Division 35 Task Force on Women, Poverty, and Public Assistance, 1998);

WHEREAS, poverty is detrimental to psychological well-being, with NIMH data indicating that low-income individuals are 2 to 5 times more likely to suffer from a diagnosable mental disorder than those of the highest SES group (Bourdon, Rae, Narrow, Manderschild, & Regier, 1994; Regier et al., 1993), and poverty poses a significant obstacle to getting help for these mental health problems (McGrath, Keita, Strickland, & Russo, 1990);

WHEREAS, accumulating research evidence indicates that the greater the income gap between the poorest and the wealthiest in a society, the higher the death rates for infants and adults and the lower the life expectancy for all members of that society, regardless of SES (Kawachi & Kennedy, 1997);

WHEREAS, the impact of poverty on young children is significant and long lasting, limiting chances of moving out of poverty (McLoyd, 1998), poverty is associated with substandard housing, homelessness, inadequate child care, unsafe neighborhoods, and underresourced schools (Fairchild, 1984; Lott & Bullock, in press), and poor children are at greater risk than higher income children for a range of problems, including detrimental affects on IQ, poor academic achievement, poor socioemotional functioning, developmental delays, behavioral problems, asthma, poor nutrition, low birth weight, and pneumonia (Geltman, Meyers, Greenberg, & Zuckerman, 1996; McLoyd, 1998; Parker, Greer, & Zuckerman, 1988);

WHEREAS, environmental factors such as environmental contaminants (e.g., lead paint, etc.), crowding, substandard housing, lack of potable water, and so forth have detrimental effects on mental and physical development that perpetuate and contribute to poverty;

WHEREAS, low socioeconomic status is associated in women with higher mortality rates and with osteoarthritis, hypertension, cervical cancer, coronary heart disease, AIDS/HIV infection, and other chronic health conditions (Adler & Coriell, 1997), and poor women are sicker and more likely to have disabilities than their nonpoor counterparts, limiting their employment options and straining their financial resources (Falik & Collins, 1996; Olson & Pavetti, 1997);

WHEREAS, men living in poverty are at high risk of violence (Reiss & Roth, 1993) and women living in poverty are at high risk of all types of violence, including sexual abuse as children, with researchers documenting reports by two thirds of poor mothers of severe violence at the hands of a childhood caretaker and by 42% of child sexual molestation (Browne & Bassuk, 1997), as well as severe and life threatening assaults as adults (Bassuk, Browne, & Buckner, 1996; Brooks & Buckner, 1996; Colten & Allard, 1997; Roper & Weeks, 1993), which presents obstacles to work and self-sufficiency (NOW Legal Defense and Education Fund, 1997; Raphael, 1996);

WHEREAS, lack of affordable health insurance, including mental health and substance abuse coverage, impedes health and well-being, and poor women are over 3 times as likely as higher income women to be uninsured: 36% versus 11 %, respectively (National Center for Health Statistics, 1995);

WHEREAS, children of teenage pregnancy and single motherhood are at high risk for a life of poverty, and birth control is not covered by health insurance plans for a significant number of women;

WHEREAS, older adults often live on limited retirement incomes, have limited prospects for future earnings, and frequently face overwhelming health care costs; 13% of older women and 20% of older persons living alone or with nonrelatives in 1998 lived on incomes below the poverty level; and 49% of older African American women living alone lived in poverty in 1998 (U.S. Census Bureau, 1999, cited in U.S. Administration on Aging, 1999);

WHEREAS, lower socioeconomic status among older adults is associated with higher rates of medical and psychological disorders, poor

older adults have poorer access to medical care, prescription medications, long-term care, and community-based care (Estes, 1995), and Medicare funds mental health care at a lower rate than medical care, and this further limits the access for older adults in poverty to mental health and substance abuse services;

WHEREAS, migrant families are by the nature of their work and life circumstances poorly served by health and mental health professionals (Portes & Rumbaut, 1996; Wilk, 1986);

WHEREAS, undocumented immigrants are vulnerable to legal actions that inhibit their access to health and mental health services, compounding issues of poverty and limited English language proficiency (Olivera, Effland, & Hamm, 1993);

WHEREAS, research focused on low-income groups including immigrants, ethnic minorities, minimum wage workers, families receiving public assistance, the homeless, migrant workers, and older women is limited;

WHEREAS, low-income groups are the targets of discrimination based on their socioeconomic status as well as other social indicators such as race/ethnicity and gender (Lott, in press);

WHEREAS, perceptions of the poor and of welfare—by those not in those circumstances—tend to reflect attitudes and stereotypes that attribute poverty to personal failings rather than socioeconomic structures and systems and that ignore strengths and competencies in these groups (Ehrenreich, 1987; Katz, 1989; Quadagno, 1994), and public policy and anti-poverty programs continue to reflect these stereotypes (Bullock, 1995; Furnham, 1993; Furnham & Gunter, 1984; Rubin & Peplau, 1975);

WHEREAS, programs that ensure that poor individuals and families have basic needs met are important in addressing the impact of poverty;

WHEREAS, ethnic strife and war disrupt the economic, public health, and social systems comprising the safety net that helps ensure basic needs are met;

WHEREAS, psychologists as researchers, service providers, educators, and policy advocates have a responsibility to better understand the causes of poverty and its impact on health and mental health, to help prevent and reduce the prevalence of poverty and to effectively treat and address the needs of low-income individuals and families by building on the strengths of communities;

WHEREAS, psychologists are ethically guided to "respect the fundamental rights, dignity, and worth of all people" (American Psychological Association, Ethical Principles of Psychologists and Code of Conduct, 1992);

WHEREAS, "psychologists are aware of their professional and scientific responsibilities to the community and the society in which they work and live" (American Psychological Association, Ethical Principles of Psychologists and Code of Conduct, 1992);

THEREFORE, Be it resolved that the American Psychological Association:

1. Will advocate for more research that examines the causes and impact of poverty, economic disparity, and related issues such as socioeconomic status, classism, ageism, unintended pregnancy, environmental factors, ethnic strife and war, stereotypes, the stigma and feelings of shame associated with poverty, and mental and physical health problems, including depression, substance abuse, intimate violence, child sexual abuse, and elder abuse, as well as advocate for the broader dissemination of these research findings.

2. Will advocate for more research on prejudicial and negative attitudes toward the poor by other persons who may individually or collectively perpetuate policies that tolerate poverty and social inequality.

3. Will advocate for more research on special populations who are poor (women and children, immigrants, undocumented immigrants, migrants, ethnic minorities, older people, people with disabilities and other chronic health conditions such as AIDS/HIV infection, and rural and urban populations).

4. Will advocate for research that identifies and learns from indige-

nous efforts by low-income people to work together to solve personal and shared problems or create organizations that advocate effectively for social justice.

5. Will recommend that where possible and appropriate socioeconomic status be identified for published reports of social sciences research.

6. Will advocate for incorporating evaluation and assessment tools and for encouraging integrative approaches such as the building of public and private community partnerships in programs addressing the issue of poverty and the poor, which psychological research has identified as effective strategies for addressing community level issues and problems.

7. Will encourage in psychological graduate and postgraduate education and training curricula more attention to the causes and impact of poverty, to the psychological needs of poor individuals and families, and to the importance of developing "cultural competence" and sensitivity to diversity around issues of poverty in order to be able to help prevent and reduce the prevalence of poverty and to treat and address the needs of low-income clients.

8. Will support public policy that encourages access for all children to high-quality early childhood education and a high-quality public school education, better equipping individuals for self-sufficiency.

9. Will support public policy that ensures access to postsecondary education and training that allows working families to earn a self-sufficient wage to meet their family's needs.

10. Will support public policy and programs that ensure adequate income, access to sufficient food and nutrition, and affordable and safe housing for poor people and all working families.

11. Will support public policy that ensures access to family-friendly jobs offering good quality health insurance, including coverage for comprehensive family planning, mental health and substance abuse services, flexible work schedules, and sufficient family and medical leave.

12. Will support public policy that ensures access to comprehensive family planning in private and public health insurance coverage.

13. Will support public policy that ensures parity with medical coverage for mental health and substance abuse services under Medicare and Medicaid and ensures for all individuals, regardless of ability to pay, access to health care and mental health and substance abuse treatment that is comprehensive and culturally sensitive, that accommodates the needs of the children of parents seeking treatment, and that addresses the special needs of older adults in poverty, including prescriptions and long-term care.

14. Will support public policy that encourages access for all children to high-quality early health care.

15. Will support public policy that ensures for all working families access to affordable, high-quality child care, which is available year round, for the full day, and for all work shifts, as well as before- and after-school care.

16. Will support public policy that provides early intervention and prevention for vulnerable children and families that enhance parenting, education, and community life so that children can develop the necessary competencies to move out of poverty.

17. Will support public policy that provides early interventions and prevention for vulnerable children and families that are strengths-based, community-based, flexible, sensitive to culture and ethnic values of the family, and that have a long-lasting impact.

*The word *family* should be understood to incorporate the functions of family members rather than their biological sex or sexual orientation, for example, lesbian heads of household.

References

Adler, N. E., & Coriell, M. (1997). Socioeconomic status and women's health. In S. J. Gallant, G. P. Keita, & R. Royak-Schaler (Eds.), *Health care for women: Psychological, social, and behavioral influences.* Washington, DC: American Psychological Association.

American Psychological Association. (1992). Ethical principles of psychologists and code of conduct. (1992). *American Psychologist, 47,* 1597-1611.

Bassuk, E. L., Browne, A., & Buckner, J. C. (1996, August 28). The characteristics and needs of sheltered homeless and low-income housed mothers. *Journal of the American Medical Association, 276,* 640-646.

Bernstein, J., McNichol, E. C., Mishel, L., Zahradnik, R. (2000, January). *Pulling apart: A state- by-state analysis of income trends.* Washington, DC: Center on Budget and Policy Priorities/Economic Policy Institute.

Bourdon, K. H., Rae, D. S., Narrow, W. E., Manderschild, R. W., & Regier, D. A. (1994). National prevalence and treatment of mental and addictive disorders. In R. W. Mandershild & A. Sonnenschein (Eds.), *Mental health: United States.* Washington, DC: Center for Mental Health Services.

Brooks, M. G., & Buckner, J. C. (1996). Work and welfare: Job histories, barriers to employment, and predictors of work among low-income single mothers. *American Journal of Orthopsychiatry, 66,* 526-537.

Browne, A., & Bassuk, S.S. (1997). Intimate violence in the lives of homeless and poor house women: Prevalence and patterns in an ethnically diverse sample. *American Journal of Orthopsychiatry, 67*(2), 261-278.

Bullock, H. E. (1995). Class acts: Middle-class responses to the poor. In B. Lott & D. Maluso (Eds.), *The social psychology of interpersonal discrimination* (pp. 118-159). New York: Guilford.

Center on Budget and Policy Priorities. (1999). *Low unemployment, rising wages fuel poverty decline.* Washington, DC: Author.

Colten, M. E., & Allard, M. A. (1997). *In harm's way? Domestic violence, AFDC receipt and welfare reform In Massachusetts.* Boston: University of Massachusetts Center for Social Policy Research.

Division 35 Task Force on Women, Poverty, and Public Assistance, APA Division of the Psychology of Women. (1998). *Making welfare to work really work.* Washington, DC: American Psychological Association. (Available from http://www.apa.org/pi/wpo/welftowork.html)

Ehrenreich, B. (1987). The new right attack on welfare. In F. Block, R. A. Cloward, B. Ehrenreich, & F. F. Piven, *The mean season: The attack on the welfare state* (pp. 161-195). New York: Pantheon Books.

Estes, C. (1995). Mental health issues for the elderly: Key policy elements. In M. Gatz (Ed.), *Emerging issues in mental health and aging* (pp. 303-327). Washington, DC: American Psychological Association.

Fairchild, H. (1984). School size, per-pupil expenditures, and academic achievement. *Review of Public Data Use, 12,* 221-229.

Falik, M. M., & Collins, K S. (1996). *Women's health: The Commonwealth Fund Survey.* Baltimore, MD: Johns Hopkins University Press.

Furnham, A. (1993). Just world beliefs in twelve societies. *Journal of Social Psychology, 133*(3), 317-329.

Furnham, A., & Gunter, B. (1984). Just world beliefs and attitudes towards the poor. *British Journal of Social Psychology, 23,* 265-269.

Geltman, P. L., Meyers, A. F., Greenberg, J., & Zuckerman, B. (1996, Spring). *Commentary: Welfare reform and children's health.* Washington, DC: Center for Health Policy Research.

Katz, M. B. (1989). *The undeserving poor: From the war on poverty to the war on welfare.* New York: Pantheon Books.

Kawachi, I., & Kennedy, B. P. (1997, April 5). Socioeconomic determinants of health: Health and social cohesion: Why care about income inequality? *British Medical Journal, 314,* 1037.

Lott, B. (in press). Low income parents and the public schools. *Journal of Social Issues.*

Lott, B., & Bullock, H. E. (in press). Who are the poor? *Journal of Social Issues.*

McGrath, E., Keita, G. P., Strickland, B. R., & Russo, N. F. (1990). *Women and depression. Risk factors and treatment issues.* Washington, DC: American Psychological Association.

McLoyd, V. C. (1998). Socioeconomic disadvantage and child development. *American Psychologist, 53,* 185-204.

National Center for Health Statistics. (1995). *Health: United States.* Hyattsville, MD: U.S. Public Health Service.

National Congress of American Indians. (2000). *Economic development.* Washington, DC: Author.

NOW Legal Defense and Education Fund. (1997, March). *Report from the front lines: The impact of violence on poor women.* New York: Author.

Olivera, V., Effland, J. R., & Hamm, S. (1993). *Hired farm labor use on fruit, vegetable, and horticultural specialty farms.* Washington, DC: U.S. Department of Education. 17

Olson, K., & Pavefti, L. (1997). *Personal and family challenges to the successful transition from welfare to work.* Washington, DC: The Urban Institute.

Parker, S., Greer, S., & Zuckerman, B. (1988). Double jeopardy: The impact of poverty on early childhood development. *Pediatric Clinician, North America, 35,* 1227-1240.

Portes, A., & Rumbaut, R. G. (1996). *Immigrant America: A portrait* (2nd ed.). Berkeley, CA: University of California Press.

Quadagno, J. (1994). *The color of welfare: How racism undermined the war on poverty.* New York: Oxford University Press.

Raphael, J. (1996). Prisoners of abuse: Policy implications of the relationship between domestic violence and welfare receipt. *Clearinghouse Review, 30,* 186-194.

Regier, D. A., Farmer, M. E., Rae, D. S., Myers, J. K., Kramer, M., Robins, L. N., George, L. K., Karno, M., & Locke, B. Z. (1993). One-month prevalence of mental disorders in the United States and sociodemographic characteristics: The epidemiologic catchment area study. *Acta Psychiatrica Scandinavica, 88,* 35-47.

Reiss, A. J., Jr., & Roth, J. A. (Eds.). (1993). *Understanding and preventing violence.* Washington, DC: National Research Council.

Roper, P., & Weeks, G. (1993). *Over half of the women on public assistance in Washington reported physical and sexual abuse as adults.* Seattle: Washington State Institute for Public Policy.

Rubin, Z., & Peplau, L. (1975). Who believes in a just world? *Journal of Social Issues, 31*(3), 65-89.

U.S. Administration on Aging. (1999). *Profile of older Americans: 1999.* Washington, DC: Author.

U.S. Census Bureau, U.S. Department of Commerce. (1999, September). *Poverty in the United States: Current population reports. Consumer income.* Washington, DC: Author.

Wilk, V. A. (1986). *The occupational health of migrant and seasonal farm workers in the United States* (2nd ed.). Washington, DC: Farm Worker Justice Fund, Inc.

References

Abelson, R., & Glater, J. D. (2004, June 17). Nonprofit hospitals said to overcharge uninsured. *The New York Times*. Retrieved June 18, 2004, from http://www. nytimes.com

Academic Human Resources. (2004). *Annual accountability report 2003–2004*. Retrieved April 12, 2006, from http://www2.ucsc.edu/ahr/about/annual_reports/ AnnualReport03-04.pdf

Academy of Achievement. (1995). *Interview: George H. W. Bush*. Retrieved May 1, 2005, from http://www.achievement.org/autodoc/page/bus0int-1?rand=19846

ADA spearheads new effort to hike minimum wage. (2002, Summer). *Good Jobs for All, 7*(1), 3.

Adair, V. C. (2002). Branded with infamy: Inscriptions of poverty and class in the United States. *Signs, 27,* 451–471.

Adler, N. E., Boyce, T., Chesney, M. A., Cohen, S., Folkman, S., Kahn, R. L., & Syme, S. L. (1994). Socioeconomic status and health: The challenge of the gradient. *American Psychologist, 49,* 15–24.

Albeda, R. (2002, September/October). Under the margins: Feminist economists look at gender and poverty. *Dollars & Sense, 243,* 30–35.

Allen, D. W. (2001). Social class, race, and toxic releases in American counties, 1995. *The Social Science Journal, 38,* 13–25.

American Psychological Association. (2005). *National Multicultural Conference and Summit: The psychology of race/ethnicity, gender, sexual orientation, and disability; What works, with whom and under what circumstances* [Brochure]. Washington, DC: Author.

American Psychological Association, Division 35 Task Force on Women, Poverty, and Public Assistance. (1997, May 16). *Implementing welfare policy to insure long-term independence and well-being*. Washington, DC: Author.

American Psychological Association, Division 35 Task Force on Women, Poverty, and Public Assistance. (1998). *Making "welfare to work" really work.* Washington, DC: Author.

American Psychological Association, Public Interest Directorate. (2000, August 6). *Resolution on poverty and socioeconomic status.* Retrieved May 29, 2005, from http://www.apa.org/pi/urban/povres.html

American Psychological Association. (2003). Public Interest Directorate. *American Psychologist, 58,* 518–520.

American Psychological Association, Urban Initiatives Office. (1999). *Forgotten voices: Conversations with women on welfare.* Washington, DC: Author.

America's Second Harvest. (2002, Spring). *Hunger Digest, 2*(1).

Angell, M. (2002, October 13). The forgotten domestic crisis. *The New York Times,* p. WK13.

Apfelbaum, E. (1999). Relations of domination and movements for liberation: An analysis of power between groups (Abridged). *Feminism & Psychology, 9,* 267–272.

Appendix B: Equity considerations in funding urban schools. (1997). *The Future of Children, 7,* 133–139.

Armour, S. (2002, April 4–17). Tough times for laid-off, low-income workers. *Spare Change,* pp. 6, 14.

Associated Press. (2003, November 2). More U.S. families hungry or too poor to eat, study says. *The New York Times.* Retrieved November 3, 2003, from http://www.nytimes.com

Atkinson, R. C. (2005). *Opportunity in a democratic society: A national agenda.* Unpublished manuscript.

Augenblick, J. G., Myers, J. L., & Anderson, A. B. (1997). Equity and adequacy in school funding. *The Future of Children, 7,* 63–78.

Aversa, J. (2005, March 2). Sharing the pain. *The Providence Journal,* pp. E1–E2.

Avery, J. M., & Peffley, M. (2003). Race matters: The impact of news coverage of welfare reform on public opinion. In S. F. Schram, J. Soss, & R. C. Fording (Eds.), *Race and the politics of welfare reform* (pp. 131–150). Ann Arbor: University of Michigan Press.

Bagdikian, B. (1997). *The media monopoly* (5th ed.). Boston: Beacon Press.

Bagdikian, B. (2004). *The new media monopoly* (7th ed.). Boston: Beacon Press.

Baker, N. L. (1996). Class as a construct in a "classless" society. *Women & Therapy, 18*(3/4), 13–23.

Baker Collins, S. (2005). An understanding of poverty from those who are poor. *Action Research, 3,* 9–31.

Banerjee, M. M. (2002). Voicing realities and recommending reform in PRWORA. *Social Work, 47,* 315–328.

Banks, M. E., & Marshall, C. A. (2005). Beyond the "triple whammy": Considering social class as one factor in discrimination against persons with disabilities. In J. L. Chin (Ed.), *The psychology of prejudice and discrimination: Vol. 4. Disability, religion, physique, and other traits* (pp. 95–110). Westport, CT: Praeger Publishers.

Barely staying afloat. (2006, May 10). *The New York Times.* Retrieved May 11, 2006, from http://www.nytimes.com

Bartle, E., & Segura, G. (2003). Welfare policy, welfare participants, and CalWORKS caseworkers: How participants are informed of supportive services. *Journal of Poverty, 7,* 141–161.

Becker, E. (2002, December 18). Mayors report requests for food and shelter are up. *The New York Times.* Retrieved December 19, 2002, from http://www.nytimes.com

Beckman, L. J., & Harvey, S. M. (2005). Current reproductive technologies: Increased access and choice? *Journal of Social Issues, 61,* 1–20.

Belle, D., & Doucet, J. (2003). Poverty, inequality, and discrimination as sources of depression among U.S. women. *Psychology of Women Quarterly, 27,* 101–113.

Bergmann, B. R. (2002, Summer). Affordable quality child care: An unmet need. *Democratic Left, 30*(1), 8, 11.

Berkowitz, B. (2002). Welfare privatization: Prospecting among the poor. In G. Delgado (Ed.), *From poverty to punishment: How welfare reform punishes the poor* (pp. 73–88). Oakland, CA: Applied Research Center.

Bernstein, J. (2003, September 26). Who's poor? Don't ask the Census Bureau. *The New York Times.* Retrieved September 27, 2003, from http://www.nytimes.com

Bernstein, N. (2005, August 15). Invisible to most, immigrant women line up for day labor. *The New York Times.* Retrieved August 16, 2005, from http://www.nytimes.com

Bettie, J. (2000). Women without class: Chicas, cholas, trash, and the presence/ absence of class identity. *Signs, 26,* 1–35.

Bhattacharya, J., Currie, J., & Haider, S. J. (2004, July). *Evaluating the impact of school nutrition programs: Final report* (USDA ERS Publication No. EFAN04008). Retrieved on June 11, 2004, from http://www.ers.usda.gov/publications/ efan04008/

Blackman, L. M. (1996). The dangerous classes: Retelling the psychiatric story. *Feminism & Psychology, 6,* 361–379.

Blank, R., & Haskins, R. (Eds.). (2001). *The new world of welfare.* Washington, DC: Brookings Institution Press.

Bohan, J. S. (1993). Regarding gender: Essentialism, constructionism, and feminist psychology. *Psychology of Women Quarterly, 17,* 5–21.

Borg, L. (2004, August 3). Less is expected of poor students. *The Providence Journal,* pp. B1, B3.

Borshuk, C., & Cherry, F. (2005). Keep the tool-box open for social justice: Comment on Kitzinger and Wilkinson. *Analyses of Social Issues and Public Policy, 4,* 195–202.

Bowen, W. G., Kurzweil, M. A., & Tobin, E. M. (2005). *Equity and excellence in American higher education.* Charlottesville: University of Virginia Press.

Broder, J. M. (2005, December 4). Health coverage of young widens with states' aid. *The New York Times.* Retrieved December 5, 2005, from http://www.ny times.com

Broder, J. M. (2006, January 2). States take the lead in push to raise minimum wages. *The New York Times.* Retrieved January 3, 2006, from http://www.nytimes.com

Brodsky, A. E. (2001). More than epistemology: Relationships in applied research with under-served communities. *Journal of Social Issues, 57,* 323–335.

Brodsky, A. E., Senuta, K. R., Weiss, C. L., Marx, C. M., Loomis, C., Arteaga, S., et al. (2004). When one plus one equals three: The role of relationships and context in community research. *American Journal of Community Psychology, 33,* 229–241.

Brooks, D. (2005, October 6). Pillars of cultural capital. *The New York Times.* Retrieved October 7, 2005, from http://www.nytimes.com

Brown v. Board of Education, 347 U.S. 483 (1954).

Bruce, N. (2001, June 15). The good fight. *The Providence Phoenix,* pp. 8–10.

Buck, P. O., Toro, P. A., & Ramos, M. A. (2005). Media and professional interest in homelessness over 30 years (1974–2003). *Analyses of Social Issues and Public Policy, 4,* 151–171.

Bullock, H. E. (1995). Class acts: Middle-class responses to the poor. In B. Lott & D. Maluso (Eds.), *The social psychology of interpersonal discrimination* (pp. 118–159). New York: Guilford Press.

Bullock, H. E. (1999). Attributions for poverty: A comparison of middle-class and welfare recipient attitudes. *Journal of Applied Social Psychology, 29,* 2059–2082.

Bullock, H. E. (2004). Class diversity in the workplace. In M. S. Stockdale & F. J. Crosby (Eds.), *The psychology and management of workplace diversity* (pp. 224–242). Malden, MA: Blackwell Publishing.

Bullock, H. E., Downing, R. A., & Limbert, W. M. (2004, August). *Becoming mobilized: Low income women and welfare rights activism.* Paper presented at the 112th Annual Convention of the American Psychological Association, Honolulu, HI.

Bullock, H. E., & Fernald, J. L. (2005). Predicting support for the elimination of the dividend tax: The role of framing and attributions for wealth. *Analyses of Social Issues and Public Policy, 5,* 20–66.

Bullock, H. E., & Limbert, W. M. (2003). Scaling the socioeconomic ladder: Women's perceptions of class status and opportunity. *Journal of Social Issues, 59,* 693–709.

Bullock, H. E., & Waugh, I. M. (2005). Beliefs about poverty and opportunity among Mexican immigrant farmworkers. *Journal of Applied Social Psychology, 35,* 1132–1149.

Bullock, H. E., Williams, W. R., & Limbert, W. M. (2003). Predicting support for welfare policies: The impact of attributions and beliefs about equality. *Journal of Poverty, 7,* 35–36.

Bullock, H. E., Wyche, K. F., & Williams, W. R. (2001). Media images of the poor. *Journal of Social Issues, 57,* 229–246.

Buss, D. (2005, September 4). Sometimes, it's not the tuition. It's the textbooks. *The New York Times,* p. BU8.

Camic, P. M., Rhodes, J. E., & Yardley, L. (Eds.). (2003). *Qualitative research in psychology: Expanding perspectives in methodology and design.* Washington, DC: American Psychological Association.

Campbell, D. (2002, Winter). Racism and the crisis of urban education. *Democratic Left, 30*(3), 6, 9, 14.

Campbell, R., & Raja, S. (2005). The sexual assault and secondary victimization of female veterans: Help-seeking experiences with military and civilian social systems. *Psychology of Women Quarterly, 29*, 97–106.

Carli, L. L. (2001). Gender and social influence. *Journal of Social Issues, 57*, 725–741.

Catholic Campaign for Human Development. (2004, January). *Poverty pulse: Wave IV.* Retrieved May 1, 2005, from http://www.usccb.org/cchd/povertyusa/povpulse.htm

Center on Budget and Policy Priorities. (2005, May 4). *What you might not have learned about the president's Social Security plan.* Retrieved May 1, 2005, from http://www.cbpp.org/policy-points4-29-05.htm

Chen, D. W. (2004, April 15). In public housing, it's work, volunteer, or leave. *The New York Times.* Retrieved April 16, 2004, from http://www.nytimes.com

Cherlin, A. J., Bogen, K., Quane, J. M., & Burton, L. (2002). Operating within the rules: Welfare recipients' experiences with sanctions and case closings. *Social Service Review, 76*, 387–405.

Chesler, P., Rothblum, E. D., & Cole, E. (Eds.). (1995). *Feminist foremothers in women's studies, psychology, and mental health* (pp. 309–323). New York: Haworth Press.

Child Nutrition and WIC Reauthorization Act of 2004. P. L. No. 108-265, 118 Stat. 729 (2004).

Children's Defense Fund. (n.d.). *The state of children in America's union.* Washington, DC: Author.

Children's Defense Fund. (2004, August). *State developments in child care, early education, and school age care, 2003.* Retrieved June 14, 2005, from http://www.childrensdefense.org/earlychildhood/childcare/default.aspx

Children's Defense Fund. (2005a, March). *Head Start basics.* Retrieved June 14, 2005, from http://www.childrensdefense.org/earlychildhood/headstart/

Children's Defense Fund. (2005b, April). *Child care basics.* Retrieved June 14, 2005, from http://www.childrensdefense.org/earlychildhood/childcare/default.aspx

Chua, K. -P. (2006, February 10). *The case for universal health care.* Retrieved April 4, 2006, from http://www.amsa.org/uhc/CaseForUHC.pdf

Ciccarelli, J. C., & Beckman, L. J. (2005). Navigating rough waters: An overview of psychological aspects of surrogacy. *Journal of Social Issues, 61,* 21–43.

Cintron-Velez, A. N. (2002). Custodial mothers, welfare reform, and the new homeless: A case study of homeless families in three Lowell shelters. In F. Munger (Ed.), *Laboring below the line: The new ethnography of poverty, low-wage work, and survival in the global economy* (pp. 148–178). New York: Russell Sage Foundation.

Citizens for Tax Justice. (2004, April 13). *Phase-in dates for the Bush tax cuts, including 2003 legislation (calendar years).* Retrieved June 2, 2004, from http://www.ctj.org/

Clay, R. A. (2001, October). Wealth secures health. *Monitor on Psychology, 32,* 78–80.

Clemetson, L. (2003, September 29). More Americans in poverty in 2002, Census study says. *The New York Times.* Retrieved September 30, 2003, from http://www.nytimes.com

Cohen, R. M. (1998). Class consciousness and its consequences: The impact of an elite education on mature, working-class women. *American Educational Research Journal, 35,* 353–376.

College costs a barrier for low-income students. (2002, January 7). *The Providence Journal,* p. A3.

Compaine, B. M., & Gomery, D. (2000). *Who owns the media? Competition and concentration in the mass media industry* (3rd ed.). Mahwah, NJ: Erlbaum.

Cook, R. (2005, May 22). Decoding health insurance. *The New York Times,* p. WK13.

Cooper, M. (2002, August 12). Jail reopens as a shelter for families. *The New York Times.* Retrieved August 13, 2002, from http://www.nytimes.com

Coplin, B. (2005, July 17). The internship divide. *USA Today.* Retrieved July 18, 2005, from http://www.usatoday.com

Cornelius, L. J. (2003). Fixing the great hodgepodge: Health care for the poor in the U.S. *Journal of Poverty, 7,* 7–21.

Corporate welfare runs amok. (2005, January 30). *The New York Times,* p. WK16.

Cosgrove, L., & Flynn, C. (2005). Marginalized mothers: Parenting without a home. *Analyses of Social Issues and Public Policy, 5,* 127–143.

Costello, E. J., Compton, S. N., Keeler, G., & Angold, A. (2003). Relationships between poverty and psychopathology: A natural experiment. *Journal of the American Medical Association, 290,* 2023–2029.

Cozzarelli, C., Tagler, M. J., & Wilkinson, A. V. (2002). Do middle-class students perceive poor women and men differently? *Sex Roles, 47,* 519–529.

Cozzarelli, C., Wilkinson, A. V., & Tagler, M. J. (2001). Attitudes toward the poor and attributions for poverty. *Journal of Social Issues, 57,* 207–227.

Croteau, D., & Hoynes, W. (2001). *The business of media: Corporate media and the public interest.* Thousand Oaks, CA: Pine Forge Press.

Davidman, L., & Tenenbaum, S. (Eds.). (1994). *Feminist perspectives on Jewish studies.* New Haven, CT: Yale University Press.

Death rate from breast cancer linked to poverty. (2002, April 3). *The Providence Journal,* p. A3.

Delgado, G. (Ed.). (2002). *From poverty to punishment: How welfare reform punishes the poor.* Oakland, CA: Applied Research Center.

DeParle, J. (2005a, September 4). What happens to a race deferred. *The New York Times,* pp. WK1, WK4.

DeParle, J. (2005b, October 2). Study finds many children don't benefit from credits. *The New York Times,* p. YT16.

Dodson, L. (1998). *Don't call us out of name: The untold lives of women and girls in poor America.* Boston: Beacon Press.

Double pinch for low-paid, chronically ill workers. (2004, September 23). *The Providence Journal,* p. A8.

Eaton, L. (2005, March 13). Bankruptcy, the American morality tale. *The New York Times,* pp. WK1, WK3.

Economic data shows Native American gains. (2005, January 6). *The Providence Journal,* p. A10.

Edelman, P. (2002, May 29). The true purpose of welfare reform. *The New York Times.* Retrieved May 30, 2002, from http://www.nytimes.com

Egan, T. (2005, May, 24). No degree, and no way back to the middle. *The New York Times.* Retrieved June 20, 2005, from http://www.nytimes.com

Eisenstein, H. (2005). A dangerous liaison? Feminism and corporate globalization. *Science & Society, 69,* 487–518.

Eisman, B. S. (1955). Attitude formation: The development of a color preference response through mediated generalization. *Journal of Abnormal and Social Psychology, 50,* 321–325.

Entman, R. M. (1995). Television, democratic theory and the visual construction of poverty. *Research in Political Sociology, 7,* 139–159.

Epstein, H. (2003, October 12). Enough to make you sick? *The New York Times Magazine,* pp. 75–81, 98, 102–106.

Epstein, W. M. (2004). Cleavage in American attitudes toward social welfare. *Journal of Sociology & Social Welfare, 31,* 177–202.

Evans, G. W. (2004). The environment of childhood poverty. *American Psychologist, 59,* 77–92.

Exhausting federal compassion. (2004, January 30). *The New York Times.* Retrieved February 1, 2004, from http://www.nytimes.com

Feagan, E. V. (1996). "Father," fetuses and abortion decision-making: The maternal ideology in Canadian judicial discourse. *Social & Legal Studies, 5,* 75–93.

Feagin, J. R. (1975). *Subordinating the poor: Welfare and American beliefs.* Englewood Cliffs, NJ: Prentice-Hall.

Fine, M. (2002). 2001 Carolyn Sherif Award address: The presence of an absence. *Psychology of Women Quarterly, 26,* 9–24.

Fine, M., & Barreras, R. (2001). To be of use. *Analyses of Social Issues and Public Policy, 1,* 175–182.

Fine, M., Burns, A., Payne, Y. A., & Torre, M. E. (2004). Civics lessons: The color and class of betrayal. *Teachers College Record, 106,* 2193–2223.

Fine, M., & Carney, S. (2001). Women, gender, and the law: Toward a feminist rethinking of responsibility. In R. K. Unger (Ed.), *Handbook of the psychology of women and gender* (pp. 388–409). New York: Wiley.

Fine, M., Torre, M. E., Boudin, K., Bowen, I., Clark, J., Hylton, D., et al. (2003). Participatory action research: From within and beyond prison bars. In P. M. Camic, J. E. Rhodes, & L. Yardley (Eds.), *Qualitative research in psychology: Expanding perspectives in methodology and design* (pp. 173–198). Washington, DC: American Psychological Association.

Fine, M., & Weis, L. (1998). *The unknown city: The lives of poor and working-class young adults.* Boston: Beacon Press.

Finn, J. L. (2002). Borders and bridges: Building new directions for the women's movement. In J. Figueira-McDonough & R. C. Sarri (Eds.), *Women at the margins: Neglect, punishment and resistance* (pp. 375–403). New York: Haworth Press.

Fiske, S. T., Xu, J., Cuddy, A. C., & Glick, P. (1999). (Dis)respecting versus (dis)liking: Status and interdependence predict ambivalent stereotypes of competence and warmth. *Journal of Social Issues, 55,* 473–489.

Fitch, R. (2005, December 28). Big labor's big secret. *The New York Times.* Retrieved December 29, 2005, from http://www.nytimes.com

Fligstein, N., & Shin, T. -J. (2004). The shareholder value society: A review of the changes in working conditions and inequality in the United States, 1976–2000. In K. M. Neckerman (Ed.), *Social inequality* (pp. 401–432). New York: Russell Sage Foundation.

Food Research and Action Center. (2002). *Good choices in hard times: Fifteen ideas for states to reduce hunger and stimulate the economy.* Retrieved June 14, 2005, from http://www.frac.org/html/publications/stimulus2002.pdf

Food Research and Action Center. (2004). *School breakfast scorecard: 2004.* Retrieved June 14, 2005, from http://www.frac.org/School_Breakfast_Report/2004/index. html

Food security: How the government measures hunger. (2004, January 11). *The New York Times,* p. WK16.

Franklin D. Roosevelt: Second inaugural address, Wednesday, January 20, 1937. (n.d.). Retrieved May 4, 2005, from http://www.bartleby.com/124/pres50.html

Freeman, L. (2002). America's affordable housing crisis: A contract unfulfilled. *American Journal of Public Health, 92,* 709–712.

Freeman, R. B. (2004). What, me vote? In K. M. Neckerman (Ed.), *Social inequality* (pp. 703–728). New York: Russell Sage Foundation.

Freudenheim, M. (2004, August 27). Record level of Americans not insured on health. *The New York Times.* Retrieved August 28, 2004, from http://www.ny times.com

Freyer, F. J. (2005, August 31). Census poverty figures show mixed results for R. I. *The Providence Journal,* p. A5.

Friedman, J. (2005, March 10). *Dividend and capital gains tax cuts unlikely to yield touted economic gains: Benefits of these tax cuts flow disproportionately to the well-off.* Retrieved April 14, 2005, from http://www.cbpp.org/pubs/fedtax.htm

Frisof, K. (2004, Fall). Affordable health care for all: Turning a dream into reality. *Democratic Left, 32*(2), P1–P8.

Frost, D. M., & Oullette, S. C. (2005). Meaningful voices: How psychologists, speaking as psychologists, can inform social policy. *Analyses of Social Issues and Public Policy, 4,* 219–226.

Furnham, A. (2003). Poverty and wealth. In S. C. Carr & T. S. Sloan (Eds.), *Poverty and psychology: From global perspective to local practice* (pp. 163–183). New York: Kluwer Academic/Plenum Publishers.

Futrelle, D., Birger, J., & Regnier, P. (2005, April 15). Making it to the top. It's never easy, but getting rich is still being done every day. All it takes is leverage. *Money Magazine.* Retrieved May 2, 2005, from http://money.cnn.com/2005/04/07/pf/getrich_0505/index.htm

Galambos, N. L., Almeida, D. M., & Petersen, A. C. (1990). Masculinity, femininity, and sex role attitudes in early adolescence: Exploring gender intensification. *Child Development, 61,* 1905–1914.

Gallo, L. C., & Matthews, K. A. (2003). Understanding the association between socioeconomic status and physical health: Do negative emotions play a role? *Psychological Bulletin, 129,* 10–51.

Gans, H. J. (1995). *The war against the poor: The underclass and antipoverty policy.* New York: Basic Books.

Gans, H. J. (1996). The so-called underclass and the future of antipoverty policy. In M. B. Lykes, A. Banuazizi, R. Liem, & M. Morris (Eds.), *Myths about the powerless* (pp. 87–101). Philadelphia: Temple University Press.

Gaus, M. (2003, September 29). Hard knocks. *In These Times, 27*(22), 3.

Gemma, A. (2004, August 26). The tortuous road to health-care reform. *The Providence Journal,* p. B5.

Geraldine Ferraro: 1984 vice presidential nomination acceptance address. (1984). Retrieved May 4, 2005, from http://www.americanrhetoric.com/speeches/gferraro acceptanceaddress.html

Gilens, M. (1999). *Why Americans hate welfare: Race, media, and the politics of antipoverty policy.* Chicago: University of Chicago Press.

Gilliam, F. D. (1999). The "welfare queen" experiment: How viewers react to images of African-American women on welfare. *Nieman Reports, 53,* 49–52.

Gold, J. (2003, Fall). Labor and health care: Wedge or squeeze. *Democratic Left, 31*(2), 8–9.

Gooden, S. T. (1998). All things not being equal: Differences in caseworker support toward Black and White clients. *Harvard Journal of African American Public Policy, 4,* 23–33.

Goodman, E., Amick, B. C., Rezendes, M. O., Levine, S., Kagan, J., Rogers, W. H., & Tarlov, A. R. (2000). Adolescents' understanding of social class: A comparison of White upper middle class and working class youth. *Journal of Adolescent Health, 27,* 80–83.

Graham, K. M. (2002). The ideal of objectivity in political dialogue: Liberal and feminist approaches. *Social Epistemology, 16,* 295–309.

Greenhouse, S. (2004, May 31). Rewards of a 90-hour week: Poverty and dirty laundry. *The New York Times,* p. B1.

Gregg, R. B. (1994). Rhetorical strategies for a culture war: Abortion in the 1992 campaign. *Communication Quarterly, 42,* 229–243.

Grossman, H. (1998). *Ending discrimination in special education.* Springfield, IL: Charles C Thomas.

Guishard, M., Fine, M., Doyle, C., Jackson, J., Travis, S., & Webb, A. (2005). The Bronx on the move: Participatory consultation with mothers and youth. *Journal of Psychological and Educational Consultation, 16,* 35–54.

Hafer, C. L., & Olson, J. M. (2003). An analysis of empirical research on the scope of justice. *Personality and Social Psychology Review, 7,* 311–323.

Halbfinger, D. M., & Holmes, S. A. (2003, March 30). Military mirrors working-class America. *The New York Times.* Available at http://www.nytimes.com

Hall, L., & Strege-Flora, C. (2002). Access denied. In G. Delgado (Ed.), *From poverty to punishment: How welfare reform punishes the poor* (pp. 189–198). Oakland, CA: Applied Research Center.

Halstead, T. (2003, January/February). The American paradox. *The Atlantic Monthly.* Retrieved February 15, 2003, from http://www.theatlantic.com

Hancock, L. (2002). *Hands to work: The stories of three families racing the welfare clock.* New York: Morrow.

Haney, C., & Zimbardo, P. (1998). The past and future of U.S. prison policy: Twenty-five years after the Stanford prison study. *American Psychologist, 53,* 709–727.

Harding, S. (1991). *Whose science? Whose knowledge?* New York: Cornell University Press.

Harper, D. J. (2003). Poverty and discourse. In S. C. Carr & T. S. Sloan (Eds.), *Poverty and psychology: From global perspective to local practice* (pp. 185–203). New York: Kluwer Academic/Plenum Publishers.

Hartsock, N. (1998). *The feminist standpoint revisited and other essays.* Boulder, CO: Westview Press.

Hasenfeld, Y., Ghose, T., & Larson, K. (2004). The logic of sanctioning welfare recipients: An empirical assessment. *Social Service Review, 78,* 304–319.

Hatch, D. (2003, October 10). Media ownership. *The CQ Researcher Online, 13,* 845–868. Retrieved April 26, 2005, from http://library.cqpress.com/cq researcher/cqresrre2003101000

Heider, D. (Ed.). (2004). *Class and news.* Lanham, MD: Rowman & Littlefield.

Hellander, I. (2003, Spring). Fix health care. Give Medicare to everyone. *Ms. Magazine, 13,* 51–52.

Henry, P. J., Reyna, C. E., & Weiner, B. (2004). Hate welfare but help the poor: How the attributional content of stereotypes explains the paradox of reactions to the destitute in America. *Journal of Applied Social Psychology, 34,* 34–58.

Herbert, B. (2002a, September 12). The invisible women. *The New York Times.* Retrieved September 13, 2002, from http://www.nytimes.com

Herbert, B. (2002b, September 16). Paying people to work, but not enough to live. *The New York Times.* Retrieved September 17, 2002, from http://www.ny times.com

Herbert, B. (2003a, February 6). Young, jobless, hopeless. *The New York Times.* Retrieved February 7, 2003, from http://www.nytimes.com

Herbert, B. (2003b, May 29). Caught in the squeeze. *The New York Times.* Retrieved June 1, 2003, from http://www.nytimes.com

Herbert, B. (2003c, October 27). There's a catch: Jobs. *The New York Times.* Retrieved October 28, 2003, from http://www.nytimes.com

Herbert, B. (2004a, June 28). A second opinion. *The New York Times,* p. A15.

Herbert, B. (2004b, July 19). An emerging catastrophe. *The New York Times.* Retrieved July 20, 2004, from http://www.nytimes.com

Herbert, B. (2004c, October 8). Working for a pittance. *The New York Times.* Retrieved October 9, 2004, from http://www.nytimes.com

Herbert, B. (2005, April 8). Black, dead and invisible. *The New York Times*. Retrieved April 9, 2005, from http://www.nytimes.com

Hernandez, D., & Leong, P. L. (2004, May 10). Feminism's future: Young feminists of color take the mic. *In These Times, 28,* 32–33.

Herrnstein, R. J., & Murray, C. (1994). *The bell curve: Intelligence and class structure in American life.* New York: Free Press.

Heymann, J. (2000). *The widening gap: Why America's working families are in jeopardy—and what can be done about it.* New York: Basic Books.

High-calorie foods often cost less. (2004, February 1). *The Providence Journal,* p. A6.

Himmelstein, D. U., Warren, E., Thorne, D., & Woolhandler, S.(2005). Illness and injury as contributors to bankruptcy. *Health Affairs, 24,* 570.

Himmelweit, S. (1999). Caring labor. *The Annals of the American Academy of Political and Social Science, 561,* 27–38.

Hobfoll, S. E. (2002). Social and psychological resources and adaptation. *Review of General Psychology, 6,* 307–324.

Hochschild, J. L. (1995). *Facing up to the American dream: Race, class and the soul of the nation.* Princeton, NJ: Princeton University Press.

Holloway, S. D., Fuller, B., Rambaud, M. F., & Eggers-Pierola, C. (1997). *Through my own eyes: Single mothers and the cultures of poverty.* Cambridge, MA: Harvard University Press.

Hong, P. (2005, October 19). College graduation rates tied to family income, new report says. *The Providence Journal,* p. A3.

Hopkins, N., Reicher, S., & Saleem, J. (1996). Constructing women's psychological health in anti-abortion rhetoric. *The Sociological Review, 44,* 539–564.

Horney, J., Greenstein, R., & Kogan, R. (2005, March 18). *What the president's budget shows about the administration's priorities.* Retrieved June 20, 2005, from http://www.cbpp.org/2-7-05bud3.htm

House, J. S. (2002). Understanding social factors and inequalities in health: 20th century progress and 21st century prospects. *Journal of Health and Social Behavior, 43,* 125–142.

Housing too high for many. (2003, September 9). *The Providence Journal,* p. A3.

Howell, P. L., & Miller, B. B. (1997). Sources of funding for schools. *The Future of Children, 7,* 39–50.

Hudson, C. G. (2005). Socioeconomic status and mental illness: Tests of the social causation and selection hypotheses. *American Journal of Orthopsychiatry, 75,* 3–18.

Hulse, C. (2003, January 9). Bush signs bill to extend unemployment benefits. *The New York Times.* Available at http://www.nytimes.com

Hunt, M. O. (2002). Religion, race/ethnicity, and beliefs about poverty. *Social Science Quarterly, 83,* 810–831.

Hunt, M. O. (2004). Race/ethnicity and beliefs about wealth and poverty. *Social Science Quarterly, 85,* 827–853.

Huntley, H. (2002, September 27). More Americans investing in stock while the market rises in popularity, the value of holdings is relatively low. *St. Petersburg Times.* Retrieved April 14, 2005, from http://www.sptimes.com/2002/09/27/Business/More_Americans_invest.shtml

Hurtado, A. (1996). *The color of privilege: Three blasphemies on race and feminism.* Ann Arbor: University of Michigan Press.

Infant mortality rate down. (2003, September 17). *The Providence Journal,* p. A2.

Institute for Women's Policy Research. (2004, August 27). *Women's earnings fall* [Press release]. Retrieved August 28, 2004, from http://www.iwpr.org

It's no insurance panacea. (2004, April 8). *The Providence Journal,* p. B4.

Iyengar, S. (1991). *Is anyone responsible? How television frames political issues.* Chicago: University of Chicago Press.

Jacob, J. M. (2005). *Factors influencing hiring decisions for welfare recipients.* Unpublished doctoral dissertation, University of Rhode Island, Kingston.

Jackman, J. (2003, Summer). What do 3.8 million have in common? Unemployment. *Ms. Magazine,* 17.

Jackson, J. P., Jr. (2004). The scientific attack on *Brown v. Board of Education,* 1954–1964. *American Psychologist, 59,* 530–537.

Jenkins, E. J. (2002). Black women and community violence: Trauma, grief, and coping. *Women & Therapy, 25*(3/4), 29–44.

Jewell, M. (2005, February 2). Study ties half of bankruptcies to medical bills. *The Providence Journal,* p. A3.

Johnson, N. G. (2003). Psychology and health: Research, practice, and policy. *American Psychologist, 58,* 670–677.

Johnston, D. C. (2005a, June 5). Richest are leaving even the rich far behind. *The New York Times*. Retrieved June 6, 2005, from http://www.nytimes.com

Johnston, D. C. (2005b, October 9). The very rich are getting even richer. *The Providence Journal*, p. F3.

Jones, S. J. (2003). Complex subjectivities: Class, ethnicity, and race in women's narratives of upward mobility. *Journal of Social Issues, 59*, 803–820.

Kahlenberg, R. D. (2004, March 16). Toward affirmative action for economic diversity. *The Chronicle Review, 50*(28), B11.

Kahne, H. (2004). Low-wage single-mother families in this jobless recovery: Can improved social policies help? *Analyses of Social Issues and Public Policy, 4*, 47–68.

Kaiser Commission on Medicaid and the Uninsured. (2005, October). *Medicaid budgets, spending and policy initiatives in state fiscal years 2005 and 2006*. Retrieved April 13, 2006, from http://www.kff.org/medicaid/7392.cfm

Katz, M. B. (1989). *The undeserving poor: From the war on poverty to the war on welfare*. New York: Pantheon Books.

Katz, M. B. (2001). *The price of citizenship: Redefining the American welfare state*. New York: Metropolitan Books.

Kaufman, L. (2002, December 24). "Temporary" homeless plan grows in New York, and so does the bill. *The New York Times*. Retrieved January 3, 2003, from http://www.nytimes.com

Kaufman, L. (2003, October 20). Are those leaving welfare better off now? Yes and no. *The New York Times*. Retrieved October 21, 2003, from http://www.ny times.com

Kaufman, L. (2005, January 8). For some homeless couples, shelter is an office floor provided by the city. *The New York Times*, p. B1.

Kawachi, I., & Kennedy, B. P. (1999). Income inequality and health: Pathways and mechanisms. *Health Services Research, 34*, 215–227.

Keister, L. A., & Moller, S. (2000). Wealth inequality in the United States. *Annual Review of Sociology, 26*, 63–81.

Keller, A. (2003, June 16). Senate has at least 42 millionaires. *Roll Call*. Retrieved May 30, 2006, from http://www.rollcall.com/issues/48_103/news/1934-1.html

Kelley, J., & Evans, M. D. R. (1995). Class and class conflict in six western nations. *American Sociological Review, 60*, 157–178.

Kelly, C., & Breinlinger, S. (1996). *The social psychology of collective action: Identity, injustice and gender.* London: Taylor & Francis.

Keltner, D., Gruenfeld, D. H., & Anderson, C. (2003). Power, approach, and inhibition. *Psychological Review, 110,* 265–284.

Kennedy, M. (2001, January 8). Access denied. Abortion may be legal, but can you get one? *In These Times, 25,* 16–18.

Kirp, D. L. (2004, April 30). And the rich get smarter. *The New York Times.* Retrieved May 1, 2004, from http://www.nytimes.com

Kitzinger, C., & Wilkinson, S. (2005). Social advocacy for equal marriage: The politics of "rights" and the psychology of "mental health." *Analyses of Social Issues and Public Policy, 4,* 173–194.

Kiyosaki, R. T., & Lechter, S. L. (1998). *Rich dad, poor dad: What the rich teach their kids about money that the poor and middle class do not!* New York: Warner Books.

Kluegel, J. R., & Smith, E. R. (1986). *Beliefs about inequality: Americans' views of what is and what ought to be.* New York: Aldine de Gruyter.

Kolata, G. (2001, April 2). Price of care higher for uninsured. *The Providence Journal,* p. A1.

Kollmeyer, C. J. (2004). Corporate interests: How the news media portray the economy. *Social Problems, 51,* 432–452.

Korteweg, A. C. (2003). Welfare reform and the subject of the working mother: "Get a job, a better job, then a career." *Theory and Society, 32,* 445–480.

Kramer, S., & Masur, J. (Eds.). (1976). *Jewish grandmothers.* Boston: Beacon Press.

Krasner, R. I. (2002, December 12). Jimmy Carter's battle for public health. *The Providence Journal,* p. B6.

Kristof, N. D. (2005a, January 12). Health care? Ask Cuba. *The New York Times,* p. A21.

Kristof, N. D. (2005b, September 6). The larger shame. *The New York Times.* Retrieved September 7, 2005, from http://www.nytimes.com

Krugman, P. (2002, October 20). For richer. *The New York Times Magazine,* pp. 62–67, 76–77, 141–142.

Krugman, P. (2004, March 12). No more excuses on jobs. *The New York Times.* Retrieved March 13, 2004, from http://www.nytimes.com

Krugman, P. (2005a, April 22). Passing the buck. *The New York Times,* p. A23.

Krugman, P. (2005b, June 10). Losing our country. *The New York Times,* p. A21.

Krugman, P. (2005c, June 13). One nation, uninsured. *The New York Times,* p. A17.

Ku, L., & Broaddus, M. (2005, May 31). *Out-of-pocket medical expenses for Medicaid beneficiaries are substantial and growing.* Retrieved June 20, 2005, from http://www.cbpp.org/5-31-05health.htm

Kurz, D. (2002). Poor mothers and the care of teenage children. In F. M. Cancian, D. Kurz, A. S. London, R. Reviere, & M. C. Tuominen (Eds.), *Child care and inequality: Rethinking carework for children and youth* (pp. 23–36). New York: Routledge.

Labor pains. (2005, January 17). *The New Republic,* 7.

Landrine, H. (1991). *The politics of madness.* New York: Peter Lang Publishing.

Lareau, A. (2003). *Unequal childhoods: Class, race, and family life.* Berkeley: University of California.

Lawless, J. L., & Fox, R. L. (2001). Political participation of the urban poor. *Social Problems, 48,* 362–385.

Lee, A., & Friedman, J. (2003, May 28). Administration continues to rely on misleading use of "averages" to describe tax-cut benefits. Retrieved June 5, 2005, from http://www.cbpp.org15-28-03tax4.pdf

Lee, J. (2004, August 10). Crucial unpaid internships increasingly separate the haves from the have-nots. *The New York Times.* Retrieved August 11, 2004, from http://www.nytimes.com

Lee, R., & Curran, L. (2003). Serving the "hard-to-serve": The use of clinical knowledge in welfare reform. *Journal of Sociology & Social Welfare, 30,* 59–78.

Lee, R. M., & Dean, B. L. (2004). Middle-class mythology in an age of immigration and segmented assimilation: Implication for counseling psychology. *Journal of Counseling Psychology, 51,* 19–24.

Legislative Analyst's Office. (2006, January 20). *Fiscal effect on California: Pending federal Deficit Reduction Act of 1995.* Retrieved May 18, 2005, from http://www.lao.ca.gov/2006/deficit_reduction/deficit_reduction_012006.pdf

Lemieux, A. F., & Pratto, F. (2003). Poverty and prejudice. In S. C. Carr & T. S. Sloan (Eds.), *Poverty and psychology: From global perspective to local practice* (pp. 147–161). New York: Kluwer Academic/Plenum Publishers.

Lens, V. (2002a). Public voices and public policy: Changing the societal discourse on "welfare." *Journal of Sociology & Social Welfare, 29,* 137–154.

Lens, V. (2002b). Welfare reform, personal narratives and the media: How welfare recipients and journalists frame the welfare debate. *Journal of Poverty, 6,* 1–20.

Leonard, A. (2004). Service learning as a transgressive pedagogy: A must for today's generation. *Cross Currents, 54,* 61–72.

Leonhardt, D. (2002, September 29). Out of a job and no longer looking. *The New York Times,* pp. WK1, WK4.

Leonhardt, D. (2005, August 31). U.S. poverty rate was up last year. *The New York Times.* Retrieved September 1, 2005, from http://www.nytimes.com

Leventhal, T., & Brooks-Gunn, J. (2004). A randomized study of neighborhood effects on low-income children's educational outcomes. *Developmental Psychology, 40,* 488–507.

Levi, M. (2001). Capitalizing on labor's capital. In S. Saegert, J. P. Thompson, & M. R. Warren (Eds.), *Social capital and poor communities* (pp. 246–266). New York: Russell Sage Foundation.

Lewin, K. (1946). Action research and minority problems. *Journal of Social Issues, 2,* 34–46.

Lewin, T. (2002, October 2). Study gives states low marks in making college affordable. *The New York Times.* Retrieved October 3, 2002, from http://www.nytimes.com

Lewis, D. A., & Monte, L. M. (2004, August). *Desperate or deviant? Trends in criminality among TANF recipients.* Paper presented at the 112th Annual Convention of the American Psychological Association, Honolulu, HI.

Lichter, D. T., Batson, C. D., & Brown, J. B. (2004). Welfare reform and marriage promotion: The marital expectations and desires of single and cohabitating mothers. *Social Service Review, 78,* 2–25.

Lichter, D. T., & Jayakody, R. (2002). Welfare reform: How do we measure success? *Annual Review of Sociology, 28,* 117–141.

Liebman, J. (2005, Summer). Toward an appropriate health care system. *Democratic Left,* pp. 8–9.

Limbert, W. M., & Bullock, H. E. (2005). "Playing the fool": U.S. welfare policy from a critical race perspective. *Feminism & Psychology, 15,* 253–274.

Lind, A. (2004). Legislating the family: Heterosexist bias in social welfare policy framework. *Journal of Sociology & Social Welfare, 31,* 21–35.

Lioz, A., & Cassady, A. (2003, July). *The role of money in the 2002 congressional elections*. Washington, DC: U.S. Public Interest Research Group.

Liss, M., O'Connor, C., Morosky, E., & Crawford, M. (2001). What makes a feminist? Predictors and correlates of feminist social identity in college women. *Psychology of Women Quarterly, 25,* 124–133.

Lott, B. (1990). Dual natures or learned behavior: The challenge to feminist psychology. In R. T. Hare-Mustin & J. Maracek (Eds.), *Making a difference: Psychology and the construction of gender* (pp. 65–101). New Haven, CT: Yale University Press.

Lott, B. (1991). Social psychology: Humanist roots and feminist future. *Psychology of Women Quarterly, 15,* 505–519.

Lott, B. (1994). *Women's lives: Themes and variations in gender learning* (2nd ed.). Pacific Grove, CA: Brooks/Cole.

Lott, B. (1995). Who ever thought I'd grow up to be a feminist foremother? In P. Chesler, E. D. Rothblum, & E. Cole (Eds.), *Feminist foremothers in women's studies, psychology, and mental health* (pp. 309–323). New York: Haworth Press.

Lott, B. (1997). The personal and social correlates of a gender difference ideology. *Journal of Social Issues, 53,* 279–297.

Lott, B. (2001). Low-income parents and the public schools. *Journal of Social Issues, 57,* 247–259.

Lott, B. (2002a). Cognitive and behavioral distancing from the poor. *American Psychologist, 57,* 100–110.

Lott, B. (2002b). *Issues of importance to low-income adults and readiness for social action.* Unpublished manuscript.

Lott, B. (2003). Recognizing and welcoming the standpoint of low-income parents in the public schools. *Journal of Educational and Psychological Consultation, 14,* 91–104.

Lott, B., & Bullock, H. E. (Eds.). (2001). Listening to the voices of poor women. *Journal of Social Issues, 57*(2).

Lott, B., & Lott, A. J. (1985). Learning theory in contemporary social psychology. In E. Aronson & G. Lindzey (Eds.), *Handbook of social psychology* (Vol. 3, pp. 109–135). Reading, MA: Addison Wesley.

Lott, B., & Rogers, M. R. (2005). School consultants working for equity with families, teachers, and administrators. *Journal of Educational and Psychological Consultation, 16,* 1–16.

Lott, B., & Webster, K. (in press). Carry the banner where it can be seen: Small wins for social justice. *Social Justice Research.*

Lu, A. (2004, March 23). Agencies say hunger on rise outside cities across region. *The New York Times.* Retrieved March 24, 2004, from http://www.nytimes.com

Luna, M., & Segal, D. (2003, March 25). Why Providence needs a living-wage ordinance. *The Providence Journal,* p. B5.

Macalister, H. E. (1999). Women's studies classes and their influence on student development. *Adolescence, 34,* 283–292.

Magnuson, K. A., & Waldfogel, J. (2005). Early childhood care and education: Effects on ethnic and racial gaps in school readiness. *The Future of Children, 15,* 169–196.

Mantsios, G. (1992). Rewards and opportunities: The politics of economics and class in the U.S. In P. S. Rothenberg (Ed.), *Race, class, and gender in the United States: An integrated study* (2nd ed., pp. 96–128). New York: St. Martin's Press.

Mantsios, G. (2004). Media magic: Making class invisible. In P. S. Rothenberg (Ed.), *Race, class, and gender in the United States: An integrated study* (6th ed., pp. 560–568). New York: St. Martin's Press.

Marks, C. (1991). The urban underclass. *Annual Review of Sociology, 17,* 445–466.

Marx, K., & Engels, F. (1938). *The German ideology* (R. Pascal, Ed.). London: Lawrence & Wishart. (Original work published 1932)

Matthews, K. A. (2005). Psychological perspectives on the development of coronary heart disease. *American Psychologist, 60,* 783–796.

McCall, L. (2003). *Do they know and do they care? Americans' awareness of rising inequality.* Unpublished manuscript. Retrieved May 1, 2005, from http://www.rci.rutgers.edu/~lmccall/

McCall, L. (2005). The complexity of intersectionality. *Signs: Journal of Women in Culture and Society, 30,* 1771–1800.

McCrate, E., & Smith, J. (1998). When work doesn't work: The failure of current welfare reform. *Gender and Society, 12,* 61–80.

McIntyre, A. (2000). Constructing meaning about violence, school, and community: Participatory action research with urban youth. *The Urban Review, 32,* 123–154.

Meritocracy in America: Ever higher society, ever harder to ascend. (2004, January 1). *The Economist*. Retrieved April 18, 2005, from http://www.economist.com/world/na/displayStory.cfm?story_id=3518560

Mettler, S., & Soss, J. (2004). The consequences of public policy for democratic citizenship: Bridging policy studies and mass politics. *Perspectives on Politics, 2,* 55–73.

Michaels, W. B. (2004, April 11). Diversity's false solace. *The New York Times Magazine,* pp. 12, 14.

Miller, S. M. (1995, March 21). Class dismissed? *The American Prospect.* Retrieved May 16, 2005, from http://www.prospect.org/print/V6/21/miller-s.html

Miller, S. M. (1996). Equality, morality, and the health of democracy. In M. B. Lykes, A. Banuazizi, R. Liem, & M. Morris (Eds.), *Myths about the powerless; Contesting social inequalities* (pp. 17–33). Philadelphia: Temple University Press.

Minimum wage enough for rent in only 4 counties, report says. (2004, December 21). *The Providence Journal,* p. A10.

Mink, G. (2001). Violating women: Rights abuses in the welfare police state. *The Annals of the American Academy of Political and Social Science, 577,* 79–93.

Mink, P. T. (2002). Foreword. In J. Figueira-McDonough & R. C. Sarri (Eds.), *Women at the margins: Neglect, punishment, and resistance* (pp. xxi–xxii). New York: Haworth Press.

Moane, G. (2003). Bridging the personal and the political: Practices for a liberation psychology. *American Journal of Community Psychology, 31,* 91–101.

Moberg, D. (2005, July 11). Class consciousness matters. *In These Times,* 28–29.

More are finishing high school. (2001, November 16). *The Providence Journal,* p. A2.

Moreira, V. (2003). Poverty and psychopathology. In S. C. Carr & T. S. Sloan (Eds.), *Poverty and psychology: From global perspective to local practice* (pp. 69–86). New York: Kluwer Academic/Plenum Publishers.

Morgen, S., & Maskovsky, J. (2003). The anthropology of welfare "reform": New perspectives on U.S. urban poverty in the post-welfare era. *Annual Review of Anthropology, 32,* 315–338.

Morgenson, G. (2005, October 23). How to slow runaway executive pay. *The New York Times,* pp. BU1, BU4.

Morin, R. (2006, March 9). Answer to AIDS mystery found behind bars. *The Washington Post,* p. AO2.

Moyers, B. (2004, June 3). *This is the fight of our lives* [Speech given at the Inequality Matters Forum, New York University, New York]. Unpublished manuscript.

Mulroy, E. A. (2002). Low-income women and housing: Where will they live? In J. Figueira-McDonough & R. C. Sarri (Eds.), *Women at the margins: Neglect, punishment, and resistance* (pp. 151–157). New York: Haworth Press.

Murphy, J. M., Pagano, M. E., Nachmani, J., Sperling, P., Kane, S., & Kleinman, R. E. (1998). The relationship of school breakfast to psychosocial and academic functioning: Cross-sectional and longitudinal observations in an inner-city school sample. *Archives of Pediatric and Adolescent Medicine, 152,* 899–907.

Murphy, J. M., Wehler, C. A., Pagano, M. E., Little, M., Kleinman, R. E., & Jellinek, M. S. (1998). Relationship between hunger and psychosocial functioning in low-income American children. *Journal of the American Academy of Child & Adolescent Psychiatry, 37,* 163–170.

Myers, M. A. (1987). Economic inequality and discrimination in sentencing. *Social Forces, 65,* 746–766.

National Center for Education Statistics. (2004, June). *The condition of education 2004 in brief* (Publication No. NCES 2004-076). Retrieved June 14, 2005, from http://nces.ed.gov/pubsearch/pubsinfo.asp?pubid=2004076

National Resources Defense Council. (2003, January). *Rewriting the rules, year end report 2002: The Bush administration's assault on the environment.* Retrieved April 14, 2006, from www.nrdc.org/legislation/rollbacks/rr2002.pdf

Nelson, T. E., & Oxley, Z. M., & Clawson, R. A. (1997). Toward a psychology of framing effects. *Political Behavior, 19,* 221–246.

Nenga, S. K. (2003). Social class and structures of feeling in women's childhood memories of clothing, food, and leisure. *Journal of Contemporary Ethnography, 32,* 167–199.

Neubeck, K. J., & Cazenave, N. A. (2001). *Welfare racism: Playing the race card against America's poor.* New York: Routledge.

New Zealand scraps workfare. (2002, Summer). *Good Jobs for All, 7*(1), 10.

NOW Legal Defense and Education Fund. (2003, December 19). *Reading between the lines: Women's poverty in the United States.* New York: Author.

O'Connor, A. (2000). Poverty research and policy for the post-welfare era. *Annual Review of Sociology, 26,* 547–562.

Opotow, S. (1990). Moral exclusion and injustice: An introduction. *Journal of Social Issues, 46,* 1–20.

Orenstein, P. (1994). *School girls: Young women, self-esteem, and the confidence gap.* New York: Doubleday.

Orloff, A. S. (2002). Explaining U.S. welfare reform: Power, gender, race, and the U.S. policy legacy. *Critical Social Policy, 22,* 96–118.

Ostrove, J. M., & Cole, E. R. (2003). Privileging class: Toward a critical psychology of social class in the context of education. *Journal of Social Issues, 59,* 677–692.

Pace, D. (2005, December 13). *Blacks, poor more likely to breathe toxic air.* Retrieved May 22, 2006, from http://web.lexis-nexis.com

Page, B. I., & Simmons, J. R. (2000). *What government can do: Dealing with poverty and inequality.* Chicago: University of Chicago Press.

Parrott, S., Schott, L., Sweeney, E., Baider, A., Ganzglass, E., Greenberg, M., et al. (2006, May 9). *Implementing the TANF changes in the Deficit Reduction Act: "Win-win" solutions for families and states.* Retrieved May 18, 2006, from http://www.cbpp.org/5-9-06tanf.htm

Payne, J. W. (2004, December 21). Dying for basic care: For Blacks, poor health care access costs 900,000 lives. *The Washington Post,* p. HE01.

Pear, R. (2003, May 13). New study finds 60 million uninsured during a year. *The New York Times.* Retrieved May 14, 2003, from http://www.nytimes.com

Pearce, D. M. (2002a). Measuring welfare reform success by a different standard. In G. Delgado (Ed.), *From poverty to punishment: How welfare reform punishes the poor* (pp. 166–186). Oakland, CA: Applied Research Center.

Pearce, D. M. (2002b). Welfare reform now that we know it: Enforcing women's poverty and preventing self-sufficiency. In J. Figueira-McDonough & R. C. Sarri (Eds.), *Women at the margins: Neglect, punishment, and resistance* (pp. 125–147). New York: Haworth Press.

Perez-Pena, R. (2005, October 17). At a Bronx clinic, hurdles for Medicaid care. *The New York Times,* p. A1.

Personal Responsibility and Work Opportunity Reconciliation Act of 1996. P. L. No. 104-193, 110 Stat. 2105 (1997).

Pew Charitable Trusts. (2003, November 25). *Most of the world still does without.* Retrieved May 17, 2006, from http://www.pewtrusts.com/ideas/ideas_item .cfm?content_item_id=1986&content_type_id=18&page=18&issue=11&issue_

name=Public%20opinion%20and%20polls&name=Public%20Opinion%20
Polls%20and%20Survey%20Results

Phillips, K. (2002). *Wealth and democracy: A political history of the American rich*. New York: Broadway Books.

Phillips, M., & Chin, T. (2004). School inequality: What do we know? In K. M. Neckerman (Ed.), *Social inequality* (pp. 467–519). New York: Russell Sage Foundation.

Phoenix, A., & Tizard, B. (1996). Thinking through class: The place of social class in the lives of young Londoners. *Feminism & Psychology, 6*, 427–442.

Physicians' Working Group for Single-Payer National Health Insurance. (2003, August 13). Proposal of the Physicians' Working Group for Single-Payer National Health Insurance. *Journal of the American Medical Association, 290*, 798–805.

Pierson-Balik, D. A. (2003). Race, class, and gender in punitive welfare reform: Social eugenics and welfare policy. *Race, Gender & Class, 10*, 11–30.

Piven, F. F., & Cloward, R. A. (1993). *Regulating the poor: The functions of public welfare* (2nd ed.). New York: Random House.

Pohlhaus, G. (2002). Knowing communities: An investigation of Harding's standpoint epistemology. *Social Epistemology, 16*, 283–293.

Potgieter, C. A. (2003). Black South African lesbians: Discourses on motherhood and women's roles. *Journal of Lesbian Studies, 7*, 135–151.

President's welfare reform package strengthens families: Remarks by the president to welfare-to-work graduates. (2003, January 14). Retrieved May 8, 2005, from http://www.whitehouse.gov/news/releases/2003/01/20030114-6.html

Price, J. H., Desmond, S. M., Snyder, F. F., & Kimmel, S. R. (1988). Perceptions of family practice residents regarding health care and poor patients. *The Journal of Family Practice, 27*, 615–620.

Prilleltensky, I. (2003). Poverty and power. In S. C. Carr & T. S. Sloan (Eds.), *Poverty and psychology: From global perspective to local practice* (pp. 19–44). New York: Kluwer Academic/Plenum Publishers.

Putnam, R. D. (2001). Foreword. In S. Saegert, J. P. Thompson, & M. R. Warren (Eds.), *Social capital and poor communities* (pp. xv–xvi). New York: Russell Sage Foundation.

Quadagno, J. (1994). *The color of welfare: How racism undermined the war on poverty*. New York: Oxford University Press.

Quinn, J. B. (2003, June 23). Tough course in tuition aid. *Newsweek, 141*, 51.

Rank, M. R., & Hirschl, T. A. (2001). Rags or riches? Estimating the probabilities of poverty and affluence across the adult American life span. *Social Science Quarterly*, *82*, 651–669.

Rank, M. R., & Hirschl, T. A. (2002). Welfare use as a life course event: Toward a new understanding of the U.S. safety net. *Social Work*, *47*, 237–248.

Reay, D. (1996). Dealing with difficult differences: Reflexivity and social class in feminist research. *Feminism & Psychology*, *6*, 443–456.

Reay, D. (1999). Fantasies of feminisms: Egalitarian fictions and elitist realities. *Feminism & Psychology*, *9*, 426–430.

Reese, E., & Ramirez, E. (2002). The new ethnic politics of welfare: Struggles over legal immigrants' rights to welfare in California. *Journal of Poverty*, *6*, 29–62.

Reid, P. T. (1993). Poor women in psychological research: Shut up and shut out. *Psychology of Women Quarterly*, *17*, 133–150.

Reid, P. T., & Vianna, E. (2001). Negotiating partnerships in research on poverty with community-based agencies. *Journal of Social Issues*, *57*, 337–354.

Relin, D. O. (2004, April 4). Won't you help feed them? *Parade*, pp. 6–9.

Remarks to the Democratic Leadership Council—Bill Clinton speech—Transcript. (1993, December 6). Retrieved April 28, 2005, from http://www.findarticles .com/p/articles/mi_m2889/is_n48_v29/ai_14891633

Reynolds, A. J., Temple, J. A., & Ou, S. R. (2003). School-based early intervention and child well-being in the Chicago longitudinal study. *Child Welfare*, *82*, 633–656.

Rice, J. K. (2001). Poverty, welfare, and patriarchy: How macro-level changes in social policy can help low income women. *Journal of Social Issues*, *57*, 355–374.

Riemer, F. J. (2001). *Working at the margins: Moving off welfare in America*. Albany: State University of New York Press.

Ritz, S. F. (2003). *The stigma of poverty: The nature and implications of everyday classism*. Unpublished master's thesis, University of Tennessee at Chattanooga.

Roach, R. (2002, December 19). Raising the spotlight on affordable housing. *Black Issues in Higher Education*, *20*, 24–27.

Robert, S. A. (1999). Socioeconomic position and health: The independent contribution of community socioeconomic context. *Annual Review of Sociology*, *25*, 489–516.

Roberts, M. L., Hite, P. A., & Bradley, C. F. (1994). Understanding attitudes toward progressive taxation. *Public Opinion Quarterly*, *58*, 165–190.

Roberts, S. (2005, September 4). In Manhattan, poor make 2 cents for each dollar to the rich. *The New York Times.* Retrieved September 5, 2005, from http://www.nytimes.com

Rollins, J. H., Saris, R. N., & Johnston-Robledo, I. (2001). Low-income women speak out about housing: A high-stakes game of musical chairs. *Journal of Social Issues, 57,* 277–298.

Rose, N. E. (2000). Scapegoating poor women: An analysis of welfare reform. *Journal of Economic Issues, 34,* 143–159.

Rosen, S. M. (1996). Dismantling the postwar social contract. In M. B. Lykes, A. Banuazizi, R. Liem, & M. Morris (Eds.), *Myths about the powerless: Contesting social inequalities* (pp. 337–347). Philadelphia: Temple University Press.

Rothman, R. A. (2002). *Inequality and stratification: Race, class, and gender* (4th ed.). Upper Saddle River, NJ: Prentice Hall.

Russell, G. M. (1996). Internalized classism: The role of class in the development of self. *Women & Therapy, 18,* 59–71.

Saegert, S., & Evans, G. W. (2003). Poverty, housing niches, and health in the United States. *Journal of Social Issues, 59,* 569–589.

Sampson, A. E., Dixit, S., Meyers, A. F., & Houser, R., Jr. (1995). The nutritional impact of breakfast consumption on diets of inner-city African American elementary school children. *Journal of the National Medical Association, 87,* 195–202.

Saris, R. N., & Johnston-Robledo, I. (2000). Poor women are still shut out of mainstream psychology. *Psychology of Women Quarterly, 24,* 233–235.

Savage, C. (2004, November 29). Military recruiters target schools strategically. *The Boston Globe.* Retrieved December 2, 2004, from http://www.commondreams.org/headlines04/1129-24.htm

Scarr, S. (1987, May). Twenty years of growing up. *Psychology Today,* p. 26.

Schein, V. E. (1975). Relationships between sex role stereotypes and requisite management characteristics among female managers. *Journal of Applied Psychology, 60,* 340–344.

Schein, V. E. (1995). *Working from the margins: Voices of mothers in poverty.* Ithaca, NY: ILR Press.

Schemo, D. J. (2002, August 9). Neediest schools receive less money, report finds. *The New York Times.* Retrieved August 10, 2002, from http://www.nytimes.com

Schoen, C., Doty, M. M., Collins, S. R., & Holmgren, A. L. (2005, June 14). Insured but not protected: How many adults are underinsured? *Health Affairs*. Retrieved June 20, 2005, from http://content.healthaffairs.org/cgi/content/full/hlthaff .w5.289/DC1

Schorr, A. L. (2001). *Welfare reform: Failure & remedies.* Westport, CT: Praeger Publishers.

Schram, S. F. (2002). *Praxis for the poor: Piven and Cloward and the future of social science in social welfare.* New York: New York University Press.

Schram, S. F., & Soss, J. (2001). Success stories: Welfare reform, policy discourse, and the politics of research. *The Annals of the American Academy of Political and Social Science, 577,* 49–65.

Scott, J. (2005, May 16). Life at the top in America isn't just better, it's longer. *The New York Times.* Retrieved May 25, 2005, from http://www.nytimes.com

Scott, J., & Leonhardt, D. (2005, May 15). Class in America: Shadowy lines that still divide. *The New York Times,* pp. YT 1, YT16–YT18.

Seccombe, K. (1999). *"So you think I drive a Cadillac?" Welfare recipients' perspectives on the system and its reform.* New York: Allyn & Bacon.

Seefeldt, K. S., & Orzol, S. M. (2004, May). *Watching the clock tick: Factors associated with TANF accumulation* (National Poverty Center Working Paper Series, 04-9). Retrieved June 4, 2005, from http://www.npc.umich.edu/publications/working-_papers/paper9/

Seefeldt, K. S., & Smock, P. J. (2004, February). *Marriage on the public policy agenda: What do policy makers need to know from research?* Retrieved March 28, 2005, from http://www.npc.umich.edu/publications/workingpaper04/paper2/

Seelye, K. Q. (2005, March 7). A flood of magazines for those awash in cash. *The New York Times,* p. C1.

Shapiro, I. (2005, March 7). *What new CBO data indicate about long-term income distribution trends.* Retrieved April 14, 2005, from http://www.cbpp.org/3-7-05tax.htm

Shapiro, T. M., & Wolff, E. N. (Eds.). (2001). *Assets for the poor: The benefits of spreading asset ownership.* New York: Russell Sage Foundation.

Shaw, K. M. (2004). Using feminist critical policy analysis in the realm of higher education. *The Journal of Higher Education, 75,* 56–79.

Shipler, D. K. (2004a, January 18). A poor cousin of the middle class. *The New York Times Magazine*, pp. 22–27.

Shipler, D. K. (2004b, February 21). Total poverty awareness. *The New York Times*. Retrieved February 22, 2004, from http://www.nytimes.com

Sicha, C. (2004, June 13). They'll always have Paris. *The New York Times*. Retrieved May 1, 2005, from http://www.nytimes.com

Sidel, R. (1990). *On her own: Growing up in the shadow of the American dream*. New York: Viking Press.

Siegel, R. J., & Cole, E. (Eds.). (1997). *Celebrating the lives of Jewish women: Patterns in a feminist sampler*. Binghamton, NY: Harrington Park Press.

Sloan, T. S. (2003). Poverty and psychology: A call to arms. In S. C. Carr & T. S. Sloan (Eds.), *Poverty and psychology: From global perspective to local practice* (pp. 301–314). New York: Kluwer Academic/Plenum Publishers.

Smith, K. B. (1985). I made it because of me: Beliefs about the causes of wealth and poverty. *Sociological Spectrum, 5*, 255–267.

Smith, K. B., & Stone, L. H. (1989). Rags, riches, and bootstraps: Beliefs about the causes of wealth and poverty. *The Sociological Quarterly, 30*, 93–107.

Solinger, R. (2001). *Beggars and choosers: How the politics of choice shapes adoption, abortion, and welfare in the United States*. New York: Hill & Wang.

Soss, J., Schram, S. F., Vartanian, T. P., & O'Brien, E. (2001). The hard line and the color line: Race, welfare, and the roots of get-tough reform. In S. F. Schram, J. Soss, & R. C. Fording (Eds.), *Race and the politics of welfare reform* (pp. 225–253). Ann Arbor: University of Michigan Press.

Sotirovic, M. (2001). Media use and perceptions of welfare. *Journal of Communication, 51*, 750–774.

Southerton, D. (2002). Boundaries of "us" and "them:" Class, mobility and identification in a new town. *Sociology, 36*, 171–193.

Stambor, Z. (2005, November). Former Irish president calls for human rights protection. *Monitor on Psychology, 36*, 26.

Stapleton, K. (2001). Constructing a feminist identity: Discourse and the community of practice. *Feminism & Psychology, 11*, 459–491.

Stark, P. (2005, December 19). The war on our children. *In These Times*, 14.

Steele, C. (2002). The represented world: Its abandoned role in social psychology. *Dialogue, 17*(1), 8–9.

Steinberg, J. (2002, May 2). Greater share of income is committed to college. *The New York Times*, p. A18.

Steinhauer, J. (2005, May 29). When the Joneses wear jeans. *The New York Times*. Retrieved June 15, 2005, from http://www.nytimes.com

Steinitz, V., & Mishler, E. G. (2001). Reclaiming SPSSI's radical promise: A critical look at JSI's "Impact of welfare reform" issue. *Analyses of Social Issues and Public Policy, 1,* 163–173.

Stevenson, R. W., & Stolberg, S. G. (2003, January 10). Bush says tax proposal will be fair for all incomes. *The New York Times*. Available at http://www.nytimes.com

Stewart, A. J., & McDermott, C. (2004). Gender in psychology. *Annual Review of Psychology, 55,* 519–544.

Stewart, A. J., & Ostrove, J. M. (1993). Social class, social change, and gender: Working-class women at Radcliffe and after. *Psychology of Women Quarterly, 17,* 475–497.

Stewart, B. (2002, November 24). There goes the neighborhood. *The New York Times*, p. WK4.

Study says 39 million in U.S. part of working poor families. (2004, October 12). *The Providence Journal*, p. A5.

Study says White families' wealth advantage has grown. (2004, October 18). *The New York Times*. Retrieved October 19, 2004, from http://www.nytimes.com

Sullivan, K. (2002/2003). Understanding the health care reform debate: A primer for the perplexed. *Social Policy, 33,* 53–58.

Terman, D. L., & Behrman, R. E. (1997). Financing schools: Analysis and recommendations. *The Future of Children, 7,* 4–23.

Terrell, R. L. (2004, March). Women on the street: Dangerous lives and premature deaths. *Street Spirit, 10*(3), 1, 20.

Thompson, R. A., & Nelson, C. A. (2001). Developmental science and the media: Early brain development. *American Psychologist, 56,* 5–15.

Tolman, D. L., & Brydon-Miller, M. (Eds.). (2001). *From subjects to subjectivities: A handbook of interpretive and participatory methods.* New York: New York University Press.

Tomes, H. (2005, September). Diversity's unmet needs. *Monitor on Psychology, 36,* 37.

Topolski, R., Boyd-Bowman, K. A., & Ferguson, H. (2003). Grapes of wrath: Discrimination in the produce aisle. *Analyses of Social Issues and Public Policy, 3,* 111–119.

Trimble, J. E., Stevenson, M. R., & Worell, J. P. (2004). *Toward an inclusive psychology: Infusing the introductory psychology textbook with diversity content.* Washington, DC: American Psychological Association, Commission on Ethnic Minority Recruitment, Retention, and Training Textbook Initiative Work Group.

The 12 percent problem. (2003, September 8). *The New York Times.* Retrieved September 9, 2003, from http://www.nytimes.com

Uchitelle, L. (2005, October 23). For Blacks, a dream in decline. *The New York Times,* pp. WK1, WK3.

Unger, R. K. (1988). Psychological, feminist, and personal epistemology: Transcending contradiction. In M. M. Gergen (Ed.), *Feminist thought and the structure of knowledge* (pp. 124–141). New York: New York University Press.

Urban, suburban teens have same worries, study finds. (2002, June 5). *The Providence Journal,* p. G7.

Urrea, L. A. (2005, October 2). City of the big gaps. *The New York Times.* Retrieved October 3, 2005, from http://www.nytimes.com

U.S. Census Bureau. (2005, September). *Income, poverty and health insurance coverage in the United States: 2004* (Publication No. P60-229). Retrieved December 5, 2005, from http://www.census.gov/hhes/www/poverty/poverty04.html

U.S. Department of Agriculture. (2004a, September). *Explaining changes in food stamp program participation rates.* Retrieved June 4, 2005, from http://www.fns.usda.gov/oane/MENU/Published/FSP/FILES/Participation/TrendsSum99-02.pdf

U.S. Department of Agriculture. (2004b, October). *Household food security in the United States, 2003.* Retrieved June 12, 2005, from http://www.ers.usda.gov/publications/fanrr42/

U.S. House of Representatives Committee on Government Reform—Minority Staff, Special Investigations Division. (2003, April). *The dividend tax cut: Fortune 100 corporate executives would reap huge financial benefits.* Retrieved March 14, 2005, from http://www.democrats.reform.house.gov/Documents/20040608091640-19649.pdf

U.S. National Health Insurance Act, H.R. 676, 109th Cong. (2005).

Vartanian, T. P., & McNamara, J. M. (2004). The welfare myth: Disentangling the long-term effects of poverty and welfare receipt for young single mothers. *Journal of Sociology & Social Welfare, 31,* 105–140.

Verba, S., Schlozman, K. L., & Brady, H. E. (2004). Political equality: What do we know about it? In K. M. Neckerman (Ed.), *Social inequality* (pp. 635–666). New York: Russell Sage Foundation.

Walkerdine, V. (1996). Subjectivity and social class: New directions for feminist psychology. *Feminism & Psychology, 6,* 355–360.

Warren, M. R., Thompson, J. P., & Saegert, S. (2001). The role of social capital in combating poverty. In S. Saegert, J. P. Thompson, & M. R. Warren (Eds.), *Social capital and poor communities* (pp. 1–28). New York: Russell Sage Foundation.

Weber, L. (1998). A conceptual framework for understanding race, class, gender, and sexuality. *Psychology of Women Quarterly, 22,* 13–32.

Weis, L. (2003). Acquiring White working-class identities: Legitimate and silenced discourse within the school. In M. Fine & L. Weis (Eds.), *Silenced voices and extraordinary conversations: Re-imagining schools* (pp. 88–108). New York: Teachers College Press.

Wells, B., & Baca Zinn, M. (2004). The benefits of marriage reconsidered. *Journal of Sociology & Social Welfare, 31,* 59–80.

Whitfield, K. E., Weidner, G., Clark, R., & Anderson, N. B. (2002). Sociodemographic diversity and behavioral medicine. *Journal of Consulting and Clinical Psychology, 70,* 463–481.

Whom do you trust? (2005, June 12). *The New York Times Magazine,* p. 17.

Wiley, M. (2002). Getting our due: Enforcing fairness in the welfare system. In G. Delgado (Ed.), *From poverty to punishment: How welfare reform punishes the poor* (pp. 155–165). Oakland, CA: Applied Research Center.

Wilson, W. J., & Aponte, R. (1985). Urban poverty. *Annual Review of Sociology, 11,* 231–258.

Winter, G. (2003, November 9). Rich colleges receiving richest share of U.S. aid. *The New York Times.* Retrieved November 10, 2003, from http://www.nytimes.com

Winter, G. (2004, December 23). Students to bear more of the cost of college. *The New York Times.* Retrieved December 24, 2004, from http://www.nytimes.com

Wolff, E. N. (2004, May). *Changes in household wealth in the 1980s and 1990s (Levy Economics Institute, Working Paper No. 407).* Retrieved April 10, 2006, from http://www.levy.org/modules/pubslib/files/wp407.pdf

Wollman, N. (2002, April). What is violence? *SPSSI Newsletter,* p. 13.

Woolhandler, S., Campbell, T., & Himmelstein, D. U. (2003). Costs of health care administration in the United States and Canada. *The New England Journal of Medicine, 349,* 768–775.

Worell, J., Stilwell, D., Oakley, D., & Robinson, D. (1999). Educating about women and gender: Cognitive, personal and professional outcomes. *Psychology of Women Quarterly, 23,* 797–811.

Worobey, J., & Worobey, H. S. (1999). The impact of a two-year school breakfast program for preschool-aged children on their nutrient intake and pre-academic performance. *Child Study Journal, 29,* 113–131.

Wright, S. C. (2001). Restricted intergroup boundaries: Tokenism, ambiguity, and the tolerance of injustice. In J. T. Jost & B. Major (Eds.), *The psychology of legitimacy: Emerging perspectives on ideology, justice, and intergroup relations* (pp. 223–254). New York: Cambridge University Press.

Wright, S. C., Taylor, D. M., & Moghaddam, F. M. (1990). Responding to membership in a disadvantaged group: From acceptance to collective protest. *Journal of Personality and Social Psychology, 58,* 994–1003.

Zafirovski, M. (2003). Conservatism, democracy, and authoritarianism. *Radical Society, 30*(2), 43–91.

Zernicke, K. (2003, November 9). What a deal! *Education Life,* pp. 23, 38–40.

Zierler, S., & Krieger, N. (1998). HIV infection in women: Social inequalities as determinants of risk. *Critical Public Health, 8,* 13–32.

Zigler, E., & Styfco, S. J. (2003). The federal commitment to preschool education: Lessons from and for Head Start. In A. J. Reynolds, M. C. Wang, & H. J. Walberg (Eds.), *Early childhood programs for a new century* (pp. 3–33). Washington, DC: Child Welfare League of America.

Ziner, K. L. (2005a, March 22). Report: Face of homeless changing. *The Providence Journal,* pp. B1, B6.

Ziner, K. L. (2005b, June 7). Drive launched to aid homeless. *The Providence Journal,* pp. B1, B3.

Zinn, H. (2003). *A people's history of the United States.* New York: Perennial/Harper Collins.

Zuckerman, D., & Kalil, A. (Eds.). (2000).The impact of welfare reform. *Journal of Social Issues, 56*(4).

Author Index

Ku, L., 122
Kurz, D., 17
Kurzweil, M. A., 116

"Labor Pains," 81
Landrine, H., 72
Lareau, A., 17
Larson, K., 115
Lawless, J. L., 13, 14
Lechter, S. L., 92
Lee, A., 79
Lee, J., 60
Lee, R., 16
Lee, R. M., 10
Lemieux, A. F., 71
Lens, V., 95
Leonard, A., 110
Leong, P. L., 5, 14
Leonhardt, D., 49, 57, 58, 62, 63, 87, 88
Leventhal, T., 55
Levi, M., 9
Lewin, K., 110
Lewin, T., 57
Lewis, D. A., 95
Lichter, D. T., 5, 104
Liebman, J., 66
Limbert, W. M., 32, 96, 104, 107
Lind, A., 114
Lioz, A., 13, 89
Liss, M., 27
Lott, A. J., 40
Lott, B., 4, 6, 7, 16, 19, 40, 46, 50, 53, 56, 100, 101, 109, 111
Lu, A., 52
Luna, M., 61

Macalister, H. E., 27
Magnuson, K. A., 117
Mantsios, G., 21, 83

Marks, C., 103
Marshall, C. A., 10
Marx, K., 81
Maskovsky, J., 104, 105
Masur, J., 34
Matthews, K. A., 69
McCall, L., 94, 107
McCrate, E., 115
McDermott, C., 107
McIntyre, A., 110
McNamara, J. M., 92, 114
"Meritocracy in America: Ever Higher Society, Ever Harder to Ascend," 88
Mettler, S., 109
Meyers, A. F., 52
Michaels, W. B., 58
Miller, B. B., 116
Miller, S. M., 49, 72, 83, 84
"Minimum Wage Enough for Rent in Only 4 Counties, Report Says," 61
Mink, G., 81, 105
Mink, P. T., 64
Mishler, E. G., 104, 106
Moane, G., 106
Moberg, D., 8
Moghaddam, F. M., 90
Moller, S., 78
Monte, L. M., 95
"More Are Finishing High School," 56–57
Moreira, V., 72
Morgen, S., 104, 105
Morgenson, G., 48
Morin, R., 6
Morosky, E., 27
Moyers, B., 48
Mulroy, E. A., 53
Murphy, J. M., 52, 120
Murray, C., 103

Subject Index

About the Authors

Bernice Lott, PhD, is professor emerita of psychology and women's studies at the University of Rhode Island, Kingston, and is a former dean of its University College. She has taught at the University of Colorado, Boulder, and Kentucky State College, Frankfort, and was a visiting scholar–professor at Brown University's Center for Research and Teaching on Women, Providence, Rhode Island; Stanford University's Institute for Research on Women and Gender, Palo Alto, California; the Department of Psychology in Waikato University, Hamilton, New Zealand; and the University of Hawaii at Manoa. She received her university's Excellence Award for scholarly achievement; served as president of the American Psychological Association's (APA's) Division 35 (Society for the Psychology of Women); and has been honored for scholarly, teaching, mentoring and social policy contributions by APA's Committee on Women, Division 35, the Association for Women in Psychology, and the National Multicultural Conference and Summit. In 1999, the University of Rhode Island awarded her the honorary degree of Doctor of Humane Letters. She is the author of numerous theoretical and empirical articles, chapters, and books in the areas of social learning, gender, poverty, and other social issues, and she is a fellow of APA and of Divisions 1, 8, 9, and 35. Her areas of interest are interpersonal discrimination; the intersections among gender, ethnicity, and social class; the social psychology of poverty; and multicultural issues. Currently, she represents Division 9 (Society for the Psychological Study of Social Issues) on APA's Council of Representatives, is a member of an Interdivisional Minority Pipeline Project working on strategies to increase the recruitment and retention of graduate students of color, and has represented Divisions 9 and 35 on the coalition of Divisions for Social Justice.

Heather E. Bullock, PhD, is associate professor of psychology at the University of California, Santa Cruz (UCSC). Her research focuses on social psychological dimensions of poverty and economic (in)justice, including discrimination against low-income women and the attitudes and beliefs that predict support for welfare and antipoverty policies. Her current scholarship examines welfare rights activism and the factors that contribute to political mobilization among low-income women. Her publications have appeared in the *Journal of Social Issues*, the *Journal of Applied Social Psychology*, the *Journal of Poverty*, and *Feminism & Psychology*. Before joining the UCSC faculty, she was an American Psychological Association (APA) Congressional Fellow with the U.S. Senate Committee on Health, Education, Labor, and Pensions—Democratic Office. She currently is a member of the APA Task Force on Socioeconomic Status.